focused

focused

Keeping Your Life on Track, One Choice at a Time

Noelle Pikus Pace

SHADOW
MOUNTAIN

To my husband, children, parents,
family, friends, and fans for allowing me
to have so many experiences
and believing in me all along the way.

We did it!

Visit us at ShadowMountain.com

The Library of Congress has cataloged this Shadow Mountain edition as follows:

Pikus-Pace, Noelle, 1982–
    Focused : keeping your life on track, one choice at a time / Noelle Pikus-Pace.
        pages cm
    Includes bibliographical references.
    ISBN 978-1-62972-013-5 (Paperbound)
    1. Pikus-Pace, Noelle, 1982– 2. Bobsledders—United States—Biography. 3. Women bobsledders—United States—Biography. I. Title.
    GV856.P55 2014
    796.9'52—dc23   2014019183

Printed in the United States of America
Publishers Printing, Salt Lake City, UT

10   9   8   7   6   5   4   3   2   1

CONTENTS

Rise above it all,

whatever holds you back, and **BECOME**

WHO YOU WANT TO BECOME.

CHAPTER 1

You Always
Have a Choice

In the blink of an eye, the dream

I had worked toward for so long was

shattered. How I chose to react

would change everything.

n 2005, I was ranked first in the world in the sport of skeleton. The Olympics were only 114 days away, and I couldn't dream of how things could be any better going into our Olympic trials. Nothing could stand in the way of obtaining my dream of winning an Olympic medal.

* * * * * * * * *

That year, I learned the power that our minds have over how we react to life. I learned that regardless of our circumstances, each moment presents us with decisions to make. It really doesn't matter what question, trial, or success we have—each traces back to a choice. At any given moment, we can choose to doubt, fear, stress, gloat, worry; to be prideful, angry, depressed, or miserable—or we can choose to move forward. We can choose to think positively. We can choose to forgive. We can choose

Thinking

If you think you are beaten, you are
If you think you dare not, you don't,
If you like to win, but you think you can't
It is almost certain you won't.

If you think you'll lose, you're lost
For out of the world we find,
Success begins with a fellow's will
It's all in the state of mind.

If you think you are outclassed, you are
You've got to think high to rise,
You've got to be sure of yourself before
You can ever win a prize.

Life's battles don't always go
To the stronger or faster [woman],
But soon or late the [girl] who wins
Is the [girl] WHO THINKS [SHE] CAN!

—WALTER D. WINTLE

to be a light and to share our talents with our friends, family, strangers, and the world. We can choose to be happy. The choice is *always* ours, and no one—no one!—can take that choice away.

As the World Cup leader, everyone expected me to win an Olympic medal. *I* actually expected me to win a medal, too. I was featured in many top magazines such as *Shape*, *People*, and *Sports Illustrated* and interviewed by some of the biggest names in television, including *The Today Show*, *NBC Nightly News*, *Prime Time*, and many more. I was twenty-two years old with the highest aspirations and the greatest possibilities at my fingertips.

At the time, my husband and I were poor college students dedicating every last penny to supporting our Olympic dream. I would travel around the world with my team for months at a time, and he would encourage me and pick me up when I was down. This was especially needed at the airport. I hated airports. An airport came to represent a place of tears and heartache where my husband and I would hug and kiss good-bye as I left for another competition. I'm sure it looked glamorous—traveling around the globe to compete with world-class athletes. But it involved hard work, long days, an incredible amount of stress, and the loneliness of being away from home.

* * * * * * * * *

Training for our U.S. Olympic trials began on October 19th, 2005. It was a sunny day, and the ice was particularly fast. I had just finished my first training run and crossed the finish line. Pleased with the way I executed the track, I dropped my feet on the ice (we don't have brakes!) to slow myself down. One at a time, my teammates joined me at the bottom of the track. We loaded our sleds into the truck, talked about our runs, and headed back up to the top of the track to do it all again.

I was so excited and anxious as I thought about being first in the world and finally becoming an Olympian. My name was called to approach the start of the track for my final training run of the day. I was smiling and joking with the members of the track crew, as I usually did, and moving around as much as possible to try to stay warm in the below-freezing temperatures. Some athletes are extremely intense when they train or compete, which is great, but I love to have fun and enjoy every minute. A few days earlier I had written in my journal, "Wow. I have an incredible job. I get to run and jump onto my stomach and go ninety miles an hour down an icy track on the side of a mountain. I absolutely love my job." Seriously, who wouldn't want to do this?

The green light turned on, and I looked forward and took a deep breath as the thirty-second countdown began to tick. I set my sled down on the ice, knowing exactly what I wanted to work on

For those who don't know, skeleton is a crazy winter sport in which an athlete sets a sixty-pound "cookie-sheet-looking sled" down on a track of ice (the same track that bobsleds use) and then sprints as fast as she can, jumps headfirst onto the sled, and maneuvers her way down a mile-long track, reaching speeds of ninety miles per hour with her chin less than an inch off of the ice. Yes, we're crazy!

during the next sixty seconds, and began to sprint forward. I sprang onto my sled, tapped my helmet on the ice to ensure I was low enough, pinned my shoulders down, tucked my arms in close to my sides, applied a small amount of pressure to my knees, and pointed my toes to make myself as aerodynamic as possible. I was focused on improving three areas I had struggled with on my previous run, and I was able to successfully fix them. It was a great run—the fastest of the day. I felt satisfied knowing I had accomplished the goals I'd set for myself that day.

I crossed the finish line and again set my feet down and stopped at the end of the track, where I unloaded my sled and waited for my team-mates to come down. One after another they came to a stop at the load-ing dock. Five of us had just finished our training runs for the day and were waiting for one last skeleton athlete to come down before we got on the truck. As we were talking about our runs and laughing about mis-takes we had made, we heard a loud noise echoing around us. I whipped my head toward the finish line and saw that a 1,400-pound, four-man bobsled was coming toward us at sixty miles per hour . . . and it wasn't slowing down. My heart felt like it would leap through my chest.

All five of us were trying to get out of the way at the same time, and I was in the back of the line. I was boxed in. There were people to my right and front and a staircase to my left. My sled began to slide down in front of me, and with the echo of the scraping ice behind me growing louder, I knew time was running out. I tried to take a step past my sled in an attempt to jump around the staircase. Right at the moment the spikes in my shoes dug into the ice to take that step, a searing pain shot through me and I was launched into the air. My body was twisted and torqued as I flew uncontrollably past our platform. I hit the asphalt twenty feet away, and the pain radiated through every inch of me. I attempted to jump to my feet but my legs gave out beneath me. I wanted to see what had just happened so I tried to jump up again, but as before, my attempt was useless. I looked down to see why my legs kept failing me. That was the moment I realized my Olympic dream was shattered. The heel of my right foot was touching the calf of my right leg. The bones of my right leg were sticking out through my sparkly pink and purple speed suit, and a pool of blood surrounded me. (My poor sparkly speed suit! I really loved that one.) In an instant, I realized that the course I had planned to take in life was altered, and I was left with a choice to make.

My teammate, LeAnn Parsley, ran to my side. LeAnn was a firefighter and had medical training. She shouted for someone to call an ambulance as she cradled my head in her hands. I'm sure that when she saw me she knew she couldn't do much for my leg, but in that moment of fear and pain, she did the one thing that I needed most—she began to pray. I don't remember the exact words that she spoke, but I

Sometimes the course we planned to take in life is altered and we are left with a single choice to make.

do remember the peace that I felt. I knew in that moment that no matter our religion, God hears all of our prayers.

The most severe pain I have ever felt came when the paramedics set my broken bones. LeAnn leaned over and warned me, "They have to stabilize your leg. Are you ready? This is really going to hurt. One,"—she

counted slowly but my mind couldn't comprehend what was about to happen—"two, three." On three, I felt my bones rip back through my skin. I was sure I couldn't take any more pain or I would pass out. I felt myself wavering in and out of consciousness. All I could think was, "I am first in the world! How can this be happening to me?" I was loaded onto a stretcher and rolled into the ambulance. Every little pebble that the stretcher rolled over shot immense pain through my body. As the ambulance doors closed, I gave way to the pain and drifted out of consciousness.

Okay, it's time to lighten it up a bit. Now for a funny story. Apparently when your bones are sticking out of your body they need to fix it really fast, so when we arrived at the hospital I was scheduled for immediate surgery. I wasn't very coherent when the doctor came to talk to me and I don't remember much of what he said, but I do remember him telling me they would be giving me something similar to an epidural, sticking a needle in my back to make me numb from the waist down. After that they would give me additional medicine to keep me asleep during surgery.

Sometime after this, I found myself groggily opening my eyes and trying to figure out where I was and what was happening. I felt an odd pressure in my leg. I looked down and saw four or five doctors standing around me, and I noticed that one of them had a hammer! They were hammering the titanium rod into my leg! I couldn't feel anything because I was still numb, *but I could see it!* I looked around and saw a doctor walking by me. "Excuse me. Excuse me!" I motioned for him to come over. He looked puzzled as I said, "I don't think I'm supposed to be awake for this!" With that, he grabbed the blue sheet that was on top of me and yanked it over my head. Now, staring at the blue around me and still feeling the pressure on my leg, all I could think to say was, "Ummm, I can still hear you!"

* * * * * * * *

Later, as I came out of surgery and was wheeled into my recovery room, I faced the realization that the thousands of hours of training, the immense sacrifices my parents and husband had made, the innumerable goals I had set along the way, my status as being first in the world, *my dream*—all of it was demolished in the blink of an eye. Tears streamed down my cheeks as the knowledge settled in my mind and heart. My leg was shattered, but the greatest pain I felt was coming from deep inside my chest.

Just then, my surgeon pushed through my door with her clipboard in hand. She glanced at me and demanded, "Why are you crying?" Her voice was flat, lacking even a glimmer of sympathy. I'm pretty sure my jaw dropped and my eyebrows rose, but she didn't seem to notice. I wanted to retort, "You get hit by a bobsled and see how *you* feel!" But I was speech-less. So she repeated, "Why are you crying?" She took a step toward me, and with an unwavering look she stated, "You can either look back and be miserable about what just happened to you, or you can move on. Your leg is broken, and feeling sorry for yourself won't change that."

Wow. Talk about telling it like it is. That was the absolute best advice I could have ever received.

I had a single choice to make. Was I going to be sad, depressed, and miserable because of what had happened to me? Was I going to be angry toward the guys in the bobsled? (Apparently the guy that was supposed to pull the brakes had never even been in a bobsled before! He didn't know when to pull the brakes!) Was I going to give up on my dream? Or would I choose to forgive? Would I choose to move forward? Would I choose to re-chart my course and get back on a path that would lead me to where I wanted to go? We always have a choice. Let me repeat this. We *always* have a choice.

* * * * * * * *

A wise man has counseled, "I am asking that we stop seeking out the storms and enjoy more fully the sunlight. I am suggesting that as we go through life, we 'accentuate the positive.' I am asking that we look a little deeper for the good. . . . Look for the sunlight through the clouds."

And so, I made a choice. Despite doctors telling me that I would not be able to walk without crutches for two to three months, couldn't jog for six months, and shouldn't even consider competing for another year, I chose to stay positive and move forward. I was back on my sled in three weeks, and I was competing on the World Cup circuit in Igls, Austria, just five weeks after the accident. Passion and a determination unlike any

I am asking that we stop seeking out the storms and enjoy more fully the sunlight. I am suggesting that as we go through life, we "accentuate the positive." I am asking that we look a little deeper for the good. . . .

LOOK FOR THE SUNLIGHT THROUGH THE CLOUDS.

–GORDON B. HINCKLEY

I had felt before drove me to believe I still had a chance to become an Olympian and represent my country on the biggest athletic stage of the world.

Despite my incredible recovery, and even though my results improved each and every race (I finished fifth in the world at the final World Cup race), I was told before the Olympic Games in Torino, Italy, that it wasn't enough. Due to my absence from competition for recovery, our national point standing fell to fourth, and we needed to be in the top three in order for me to qualify. To put it in the simplest terms, the 2006 Olympics were absolutely heart-wrenching for me to watch, idly incapable of doing anything while knowing I would have a very good shot at winning a medal if I could only compete. I was once again broken, but the lesson I had learned just 114 days before about optimism and moving forward gave me strength and courage to believe that this too would pass.

* * * * * * * * *

We might break down a bit when trials come. That's okay. Our hearts will probably hurt when life seems unfair. It's only natural. But a favorite scripture of mine helps to calm the hurt that will inevitably come:

For healing to take place we must recognize that we always have a

"*Peace* I LEAVE WITH YOU, my peace I give unto you: Not as the world giveth, give I unto you. **Let not your heart be troubled,** *neither let it be afraid.*" —John 14:27

choice. No matter how we are mistreated, no matter what obstacles, pains, or sorrows we face, no matter what tomorrow brings, we can always choose a reaction that gets us moving forward. I am grateful for an unsympathetic doctor that opened my eyes and reminded me that I had a choice to make. She reminded me that I *always* have my agency, my ability to choose. It is up to me to choose my path. It is up to me to forgive, to be positive, and to press on along the course that will lead me to become the woman I want to be.

Where are your choices leading you? Do not allow your circumstances to dictate who you are or where you are going. Rise above whatever holds you back, and choose to become who you want to be.

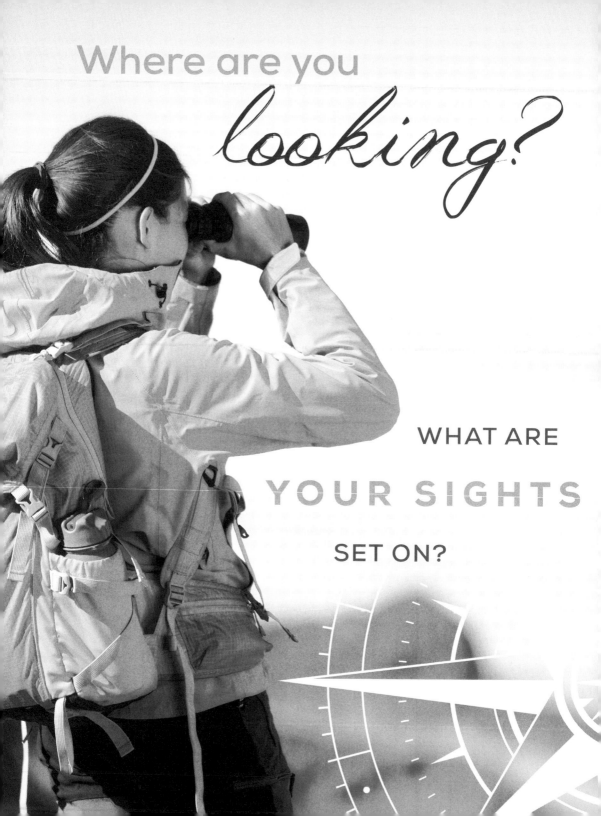

CHAPTER 2

Where You Look Is Where You Go

Standing at the top of the track before

my run, I knew where I needed to go. . . .

I knew the destination I wanted to reach,

but I didn't know how to get there.

The most dangerous skeleton track in the world is found in eastern Germany just five miles from the Czech border. As a twenty-year-old competing for the first time against the world's highest-level athletes on the World Cup circuit, I was petrified about taking it on.

We landed in Munich and had an eight-hour drive to our destination. As we drove through Dresden, which is an hour southwest of the track, I couldn't help but wonder if the scenery was an omen of what was to come. It was drizzling, the trees were bare, and many buildings were demolished from the wars and bombs of many years ago. Thick cloud coverage laid a gray blanket across everything in view. Black charred remains were all that was left of a once ornate cathedral. Windows were shattered and bricks still lay scattered on the ground below. I couldn't help but imagine how the city had once looked. Full of life, light, and color, I'm sure.

Reality set in as we left Dresden and approached the little town of Altenberg, Germany, where the track was. My hands were clammy, my heart was racing, and I'm pretty sure that if my seat belt wasn't strapping me in to the van, my fight-or-flight response would have encouraged me to fly.

Most skeleton tracks have one or two difficult curves that you need to carefully drive your sled through to be safe. This particular track is much different. One of my teammates, Chris, approached me and said, "This is seriously the most dangerous track in the world." That definitely did not help. He continued, "Just make sure that you pay attention in curve four, because it is easy to hit the roof and crash. If you get curve four, you'll be fine."

Right then another teammate chimed in, "No way, curve four is nothing compared to curve nine. Curve nine will flip you onto your back if you're not prepared, and then you're toast!"

A third teammate then said, "Don't worry about those curves, curve ten and twelve are the ones you should worry

Most skeleton tracks have one or two difficult curves that you need to carefully drive your sled through to be safe.

about! You need to be firm in your steers in those curves. They are harder than . . ."

The conversation left me drifting away in my own thoughts of doom and gloom. Apparently there were five or six curves in Altenberg that could cause pain. I had confidence in my ability. I mean, I was on the World Cup team. I was one of the best athletes in *the world*. I was supposed to suck it up, dismiss my fear, and just go with the flow, right? I didn't want the others to see me as weak or young, so I tried to put on my tough face and act unafraid.

* * * * * * * *

We arrived at the track, and I slowly changed into my extremely thin spandex speed suit. I cushioned my elbows with volleyball knee pads and placed cut-up pieces of a foam camping mattress under my speed suit to protect my calves, arms, and shoulders. This was my high-tech effort to alleviate the pain I thought could be coming.

As I stood at the top of the track and waited for my turn I began to shake, my heart nearly leaping out of my chest. I tried to play down my nervousness and acted like I was merely shaking from the cold. I even acted excited so that my competitors wouldn't see my fear. Mind games are definitely a part of competition. I was the youngest on the team, but I wanted desperately to be the best and to cover up any insecurity that I had.

A girl from Japan that had been on the World Cup circuit for many years was called to the start. She placed her sled on the ice, sprinted down the icy chute, jumped onto her sled, and disappeared past the crest into curve one. I watched her time ticking as she navigated the course. About halfway through her run the announcer came on the broadcast,

MIND GAMES

are definitely a part
of competition.

Skeleton athletes typically set our sleds down and take off in a full sprint before leaping onto our stomachs and navigating our way down the icy course.

"*Achtung! Achtung! 81! 81 im die bahn!*" 81 meant that the athlete had crashed, come off of her sled, and would need medical attention. The paramedics and ambulance immediately rushed her away to the hospital. Just then Chris ran up to me and said, "No matter what you do, do NOT get in the *Krankenwagen*! They don't have doctors in this town. They take you to the vet! We don't know when we'll see you again!" *Krankenwagen* is "ambulance" in German. I'm pretty sure that's not the typical first word people learn in a foreign language, but it was mine.

Okay, I thought as I inhaled a deep breath and held it, *curves four, nine, ten, twelve, fifteen? What am I doing?! Oh my goodness. Maybe I shouldn't go down today. Maybe I'll just wait and go tomorrow. No, Noelle . . . you can do this! Or can I? Pull yourself together! You'll be fine. Just go with the flow. How bad can it really be? You're a great athlete. You can do this! What am I doing here?!* As you can see, I was having quite an internal battle with myself.

There was one more girl up before me. She was a World Cup medalist from Canada, so I knew she would be fine. She had to be fine, right? Still shaking, I watched the clock intently as she maneuvered her way down the track. Halfway through, once again, the announcer shouted, "*81! 81 im die bahn!*" The Canadian medalist had crashed. She was loaded onto the *Krankenwagen*, and we didn't see her again for three days. Three days!

My eyes were as wide as my terrified three-year-old son's on a roller coaster. My jaw hung in disbelief. *What in the world am I doing here?! Forget what I said before, Noelle. You shouldn't be doing this.*

The green light flashed on and brought me back to reality. Other athletes were watching and waiting for me. I had only thirty seconds to set my sled down and go. I adjusted my elbow pads to ensure they would protect me. Skeleton athletes typically set our sleds down and take off in a full sprint before leaping onto our stomachs and navigating our way down the icy course. This time was much different. I slowly placed one foot in front of the other, holding the weight of the sled back in an effort to keep my momentum—and the possibility of a crash—to a minimum. Once I passed the crest there was no turning back. I lowered my body onto my sled and began to timidly and fearfully navigate the course.

Curve one and two came and went. *Okay. Okay! I'm doing it! I'm going to be okay!* The moment I had that thought, however, I hit a wall on the exit of curve three, which shot me to the roof and flipped me onto my back. *I'm not doing it! I knew this would happen! What am I doing?!* I was determined to keep gripping on to my handles as tightly as was humanly possible. Fortunately, the next curve went in the other direction and flipped me back onto my sled. It all happened in less than a second, and I wondered if that had really just happened. Before my mind could catch up to the speed at which my body was traveling, I was flying through curves five through eight. Once again I was tossed onto my back on the exit of curve nine. *Holy smokes! I'M GOING TO DIE!* As I slid on my back for about sixty meters, my grip on my sled tightened and

I somehow found the strength to turn it over just in time to enter curve ten, otherwise known as *Kreisel*.

Kreisel, the second word I learned in German, means "circle." This *Kreisel* is one of the largest curves in the world. It is a 360-degree turn. In the sport of skeleton, each curve puts two to three "pressures" against our bodies—up to six G's pushing against us. In other words, the force against us makes the weight of our body as much as six times as heavy. We try to counteract the pressures by steering the sled up or down as needed. As I entered this curve, the pressure immediately suctioned my head to the ice. I felt an incredible force against my head, neck, and body. My mind went blank. I was going so fast and was so drained of energy that my athletic instinct froze and I forgot what I was supposed to do. I decided doing nothing was better than possibly making it worse. I had just made it out of some really difficult curves. I truly doubted this curve was any different. I just had to hold on to my sled and cross the finish line. My sled followed the physics of the course. It rose and fell with the pressure of the curve. I watched helplessly as my sled rose dangerously close to the wooden roof and slid back down to the bottom of the curve. *Maybe I should do something?* But before I could make a decision I rose back up toward the roof and again slid back down to the belly. In that instant I realized what would inevitably follow. I was going to rise one final time before reaching the curve's exit. As I strained to see against the G forces on my neck that a seventy-mile per hour curve will bring, I caught a glimpse of the scarred wooden panel on the roof. I watched it draw near and my mind filled with fear. *Don't hit the roof. Don't hit the roof! Please don't hit the roof!*

Time stood still in the moments before the collision. Suddenly a searing pain shot through the left side of my body. I knew the worst was yet to come as I was launched uncontrollably through the air. I saw only white ice and glimpses of pine trees until my back slammed against the ice ten feet below. My sixty-pound sled landed on my chest. I couldn't breathe. I was trapped. Sheer panic shot through every muscle, organ, and thought in my body. I thrust the sled out in front of me and slid through the next curves on my back. Breath had yet to fill my lungs as the pain from the shards of ice began to rip through the thin speed suit covering my arms, back, and shoulders. The track is refrigerated, and the ice in it feels similar to the ice crystals that form inside of a freezer, jagged and coarse. I rolled onto my stomach to alleviate the pain on my back and calves and pressed my hands, knees, and feet into the ice in an effort to stop. My knees began to throb, and I knew they were bleeding. Seconds that felt like hours passed until I finally came to a halt. I gasped for breath, sucking in as much air as my lungs and closed-off throat would allow. It wasn't enough. In the distance I could see the silhouettes of what must have been the Altenberg paramedics, and I imagined the *Chariots of Fire*

The track is refrigerated, and the ice in it feels similar to the ice crystals that form inside of a freezer, jagged and coarse.

theme song playing as they ran in what appeared to be slow motion. My body ached as I tried to stand. The pounding heartbeat I had felt deep inside my chest at the top of the track had shifted and now throbbed in a very localized spot on my elbow. A large hole in my black suit made way for bright red blood to drip onto the pristine ice below me. My high-tech padding hadn't worked out too well for me—I looked back up the icy track and saw remnants of camping foam and volleyball knee pads strewn everywhere. Air slowly began to fill my lungs as the paramedics arrived and attempted to help me toward the *Krankenwagen*.

"Nein Krankenwagen." I forced air out, trying to speak. The paramedics continued to guide me out of the track and toward the ambulance. *"Nein Krankenwagen bitte."* I said as normally as I could. *"Alles gut."* There you have it. That was the extent of my German. "No ambulance please. I'm good." I cradled my elbow as gently as I could, hoping to hide the injury beneath. They pointed to different areas of my

body that were clearly not okay and continued to insist that I enter the *Krankenwagen*. Fortunately, one of my teammates came running to my side and confirmed to the paramedics that I was okay. Reluctantly they let me go, and my teammate escorted me back to the top of the track, where my wounds were assessed and bandaged. It was there that I first pondered the critical lesson I had learned in the hundredths of a second that preceded the accident.

Standing at the top of the track before my run, I knew where I needed to go. I needed to go down the track and cross the finish line. That was it. I knew the destination I wanted to reach, but I didn't know how to get there. I knew that once I was in the curves, I would be in danger if I didn't control the pressures around me. I had received guidance and warnings from teammates, but I hadn't prepared myself enough to get through the difficult times.

I was thrown into a situation I had not prepared for, and it caught me off guard. I was knocked off my course and didn't know how to get back on the right track. Not wanting to do something wrong or make a mess of the situation, I decided to just "go with the flow." I chose to do nothing, thinking that I was strong enough to get myself out of a rough situation based solely on my own knowledge. I knew who I was—a World Cup athlete competing against the best athletes in the world—but I didn't understand that being at that level didn't mean I had to be perfect. I had felt that I wasn't good enough and that I needed to be more. I had felt that the expectations of me were bigger than who I actually was, but I wasn't about to let others know I was afraid. And so instead of seeking further guidance, I rose and fell with the pressures in the curve that could have easily been executed had I been prepared.

Once I made a mistake on that first pressure in the massive curve, it was incredibly difficult to backtrack and correct my course, although it was still possible. I knew I probably wasn't where I should be on the track, but I didn't see the further danger around the corner. By the third and final pressure in that curve, the situation felt beyond my control. I was scared. I didn't know how to escape. I knew I should have better controlled the first pressure of the curve, but by then it was too late. I was just backpedaling, trying to make up for mistakes I had made earlier.

As I rose up the side of the track with that final pressure, time seemed to stop. It was too late to escape. My sights were set solely on the roof of this massive curve as I repeated over and over, "Don't hit the roof. Don't hit the roof!" I was looking right at the roof, and I hit it.

✳ ✳ ✳ ✳ ✳ ✳ ✳ ✳ ✳

Where are you looking? What are your sights set upon? Where are your goals leading you? We have been blessed with the ability to know right from wrong. That feeling of being uncomfortable in a situation or the brief thought that says we shouldn't be doing something, watching something, or thinking something is more than just an emotion.

In life, we will all make mistakes. Sometimes we don't recognize them for days, months, or even years. At times we recognize those mistakes immediately but ignore them, and by the time we realize what a mess we have gotten ourselves into, we are two or three pressures into the curve and we feel there is no escape. Sometimes we hit the roof and come out bleeding and broken. That is when it is time to pick ourselves up, fix our mistakes, and move forward once again. If we see the roof coming, however, we can shift our gaze to where we would *like* to go, rather than where we don't want to crash, and we can continue on our course and safely cross the finish line.

My challenge to you is to chart your course. Set your sights ahead of you. Make a plan. Where do you want to be physically, spiritually, and emotionally in a year? in five years? Choose your destination, and then set small goals for yourself that will lead you to your finish line.

We can heed this counsel by setting small goals to work on each week. I like to focus on three goals at a time. Remind yourself of these goals each morning when you wake up, and be committed to reaching

Like the vital rudder of a ship, we have been provided a way to determine the direction we travel. . . . Our purpose is to steer an undeviating course in that direction. A man without a purpose is like a ship without a rudder—never likely to reach home port. To us comes the signal: Chart your course, set your sail, position your rudder, and proceed.

—Thomas S. Monson

them. As I have charted my course, in sports and in other aspects of my life, I have come to understand and accept that our courses will inevitably run through unexpected challenges along the way. When these challenges, trials, or mistakes come up, I have to slow down, correct the issues, and then re-chart my course to get to where I want to be. Expect the same in your own course, and be forgiving of yourself and the mistakes you make. Be positive through the aches and pains that might set you back.

My teammates told me to "pay attention," "be prepared," and "be firm." We must all pay attention to the temptations and trials that distract us from our course and potentially harm us. We have choices every single day that can lead us along our charted course or away from it. Be prepared by knowing now who you are and what you stand for. Then, when a situation arises that makes you feel uncomfortable, weak, or incapable, you will easily steer your way through. Finally, be firm in your decisions and beliefs. Be firm and dedicated to your goals.

If we do this, then at the end of our lives we will be able to echo what is written in 2 Timothy 4:7.

"I have fought a

good fight,

I have finished

my course,

I have kept the

FAITH."

—2 Timothy 4:7

BE *fearless* AND **love** YOURSELF FOR WHO YOU ARE.

CHAPTER 3

My

Competition

> Day after day, race after race, I was discouraged. . . . I was so focused on my competition that I couldn't allow myself to be happy.

have always believed I could do anything. Why not? If there was something I didn't do, someone else would! If I didn't become a doctor, a baker, or a builder, someone else would dream of becoming it and they would do it. Why not me? It was just a matter of figuring out exactly what my dream was and making it happen. Well, I loved sports, so that was an obvious direction to go in. I hadn't always loved sports. Actually, I didn't know they existed until I was eleven years old. My mom had had a profound dream to have a little ballerina with a pink frilly tutu in the family. I guess not all dreams come true. I danced from the age of three until the day that a friend of mine asked me to sign up for fast-pitch softball. Off came the slippers and on came the cleats.

I absolutely loved softball. I loved spending hours in the backyard pitching with my dad. I liked the pressure of being on the mound as the final inning closed in and the score was tied. It all came down to how well I, the rest of my team, and the batter could handle the pressure. It was a thrill for me to compete and to fight back the butterflies every time I was asked to perform my best. Over the next few years I fell in love with basketball, soccer, and track and field. I wanted to be the best at whatever I did. I wanted to see what I was capable of. I entered high school knowing I needed to begin to think about what I wanted to do for the rest of my life. My parents had instilled in me the priority of going to college, so for me it wasn't an option not to go. Although I loved softball and all of the other sports I played, I had a true passion for track and field. I loved the variety of talents combined in one arena. There were so many different athletes with different body shapes and different personalities excelling in different events. The athletes on the track team seemed so positive, happy, and fun to be around that they made me want to be a better athlete and person. I decided I wanted to go to college on a track and field scholarship, and I knew I would have to work hard to make it happen. I wasn't the fastest sprinter, but I really excelled in most of the field events, so my coach suggested I focus on becoming a heptathlete. A

heptathlete competes in seven different track and field events over two days. These events include high jump, long jump, javelin, shot put, 100-meter hurdles, 200-meter sprint, and the 800-meter run. I loved the competitions. I loved the variety of events, the challenge of learning the techniques, and building the speed and strength

I loved the variety of events, the challenge of learning the techniques, and building the speed and strength necessary to succeed.

necessary to succeed. I recognized that my confidence was built as I pushed my fears aside and allowed myself to fail or make mistakes on my way to becoming better.

It was during this time, in the middle of my junior year of high school, that Steve Revelli, my track coach, approached me and asked if I wanted to try bobsledding. Random, right? He mentioned that the coaches were trying to recruit athletes with "speed and power" and were specifically looking for heptathletes. I lived an hour south of where the 2002 Olympic Games would take place in Salt Lake City, Utah. Coach Revelli was helping out with the development bobsled program in Park City, Utah, just twenty minutes from Salt Lake City. The only thing I had ever known about bobsledding came from the movie *Cool Runnings*. The guys in that movie seemed to have a lot of fun doing it, so I figured I would give it a try. When I arrived at the icy track later that week, a man introduced himself as the junior development bobsled coach. He handed me some lacrosse padding for my shoulders and a helmet for my head. He then walked over to the start, where a bobsled was waiting and a driver was ready to go. I was told to grasp the handles on the back of the bobsled, push the sled as far as I could, jump into the back seat, and hold on tight. I didn't realize it at the time, but once I sat down in the bobsled and slid down the track, my life would never be the same. I was hooked. I absolutely loved it.

As a sixteen-year-old just starting out, I was responsible only for pushing, jumping in, holding on tight, and pulling the brakes of the bobsled. Eventually I began to drive the massive sled down the track. The following year I was encouraged to try the sport of skeleton. A little cookie sheet-looking sled lay at the entrance to the halfway point of the same icy track used for bobsled and luge. I had never seen a skeleton sled before, so I was very curious when my coach gave me a helmet and told me to lie down on it on my stomach. I thought he was joking. When I saw the expression on his face I knew he meant it, so I did what I was told. He asked me to grab the sled handles at the sides of my body near my hips and told me to hold on tight. Without any further instruction, he pushed me off down the hill. I didn't even know what this crazy sport was called! To this day, I vividly remember hitting every wall and screaming for my life. My shrieks could be heard throughout the Olympic Park. About thirty seconds into my run, however, I realized I was okay. Soon my shrieks turned into squeals of excitement. "Wahoo! This is AWESOME!" I yelled as I crossed the finish line. Eventually

I was able to take my sixty-pound sled to the top of the track, lay it on the ice, sprint as fast as I could while holding onto one of the handles, jump onto my stomach with my chin just an inch off of the ice, and steer my way down the mile-long track while reaching speeds of ninety miles per hour. I fell in love with skeleton and never looked back. I decided to dedicate myself to the sport with the hope of one day representing my country in the Olympics.

✳ ✳ ✳ ✳ ✳ ✳ ✳ ✳

I received a full scholarship to compete in track and field at Utah Valley University and continued to learn and progress toward a bachelor's degree in community health. I really enjoyed learning about the human body through classes such as anatomy, kinesiology, and biomechanics. I loved to learn how the body moved and why we are able to do the things that we do.

As I continued to compete in track and field and attend school, I qualified to compete on the U.S. National Skeleton Team. I had the opportunity to travel around the world and compete against the best athletes from every nation. I had one goal: I wanted to beat them all.

I was an experienced athlete, representing a Division I university, so I knew how to compete. I knew what it meant to beat my competition . . . or so I thought. During training I paid attention to see which athletes were the fastest. I would watch them out of the corner of my eye as they warmed up, take note of how they acted, and even notice what they ate before they slid. In my first few years of sliding, my equipment was very basic, and I often found myself wishing that I had what others had and could do what they did. If my times were slow, I blamed it on my equipment being slow. I found myself comparing speed suits and sprinting spikes, constantly wishing that I had what they had. I wasn't the fastest sprinter, so I constantly put myself down for my lack of speed at the top of the track. I would stand at the starting line and think about my competition. *You're going down. I'm going to go so fast that you're not going to know what hit you.* Yes, I would trash talk. I have never been the kind of person to trash talk out loud, but I definitely have made my fair share of remarks in my mind. Day after day, race after race, I was discouraged. I would come in fifth, eleventh, or sometimes even second, but I always considered it a failure. Someone had beaten me. I wanted to turn heads and impress the other athletes, my coaches, and coaches from other nations. I wanted them to see me as someone to look up to and someone to envy. I was so focused on my competition that I couldn't allow myself to be happy. I never tried to see what positive attributes I had. I wasn't honest with myself about what changes I needed to make in order to improve my abilities.

Who is your competition? Take a minute to think about it. Who are you constantly trying to outperform, outdo, or impress? Why do you wear what you wear? Why do you say what you say? Who do you look up to and why?

✻ ✻ ✻ ✻ ✻ ✻ ✻ ✻

Now let's fast forward twelve years. I was preparing to compete at the 2014 Winter Olympic Games in Sochi, Russia, and my focus had drastically changed over the years. I now focused on my strengths. *I am one of the best skeleton drivers in the world. My speeds are rarely beat. I have the ability to slow time down in my mind and see every single inch of ice as I fly down the icy chute at ninety miles per hour. I understand how my*

One of the greatest lessons we can learn in this life is that our fiercest competition will always be with ourselves. Focusing on my strengths and improving my weaknesses has propelled me forward to get to where I want to go.

sled and body will react to the physics of each curve as I experience intense forces of pressure. I can quickly alter my steering to ensure a safe and fast run. I learned to be honest with myself. I knew that I had weaknesses. My start, the forty-meter sprint, had always been an area that had inhibited my performance. Other athletes were faster and more agile in the beginning portion of the track. That was okay. I didn't have their talents, and they didn't have mine.

I now competed on a sled that was perfect for me. My husband, Janson, had designed it, and I was confident in its ability. Other athletes had brand new equipment the day of the race. It was the Olympics, after all, and the best would be required. Other nations had millions of dollars invested into research and development of equipment in order to ensure that their athletes had the best opportunity for success. I didn't let it bother me. I had confidence that what I had was good enough. It had gotten me to where I was, and it would get me to where I wanted to go. I never paid attention to any of the other athletes. Not because I was trying to avoid them or prove a point of any kind, but because each race truly was my moment. I wanted to take it all in, enjoy every minute, and learn what my best was. I wanted to simply but definitively give my best.

I want to ask you one more time: who is your competition?

When I first began competing, my competition was everyone else. I compared my weaknesses to their strengths, belittling my own strengths and discounting my successes. I focused on who they were and where they were going. I wanted what they had and couldn't see past my own insecurities. One of the greatest lessons we can learn in this life is that our fiercest competition will always be with ourselves.

As we compare ourselves with others, we set ourselves up for disappointments throughout our lives. Each one of us is uniquely shaped, talented, beautiful, and capable of greatness. No one else can equally provide what you have to offer to this world and to those around you. As long as we strive to develop our talents to the best of our ability and not compare them to another's, we will most definitely partake of happiness and make this world a better place to live.

Comparing myself to other athletes, even in the world of competition, never brought success to my career. It only brought discouragement, a lack of self-worth, and a constant flow of negative thoughts. A woman I admire has said, "We are doing well when we seek to improve ourselves and do our best. We are doing well when we increase faith and personal righteousness, strengthen families and homes, and seek out and help others who are in need. . . . When we have done our very best, we may still experience disappointments, but we will not be disappointed in ourselves."

Be fearless and love yourself for who you are and what you can offer. Share your talents, whatever they may be, with those around you. Be humble when you recognize you have a gift, and continue to develop it. Help and encourage others as they try new things and develop their talents. Don't be afraid for them to succeed. Their success cannot diminish

We are doing well when we seek to improve ourselves and do our best. We are doing well when we increase faith and personal righteousness, strengthen families and homes, and seek out and help others who are in need. . . .

When we have done our very best, we may still experience disappointments, but we will not be disappointed in ourselves.

—JULIE B. BECK

your talents unless you allow it to. Compliment yourself when you do something praiseworthy. Compliment others as well. Be honest with yourself about your weaknesses, and strive to make them stronger. Don't

strengthen your weakness in order to beat someone else, but strengthen them to become the best version of yourself. Finally, and most important, dare to be you! It is very easy to forget that this life is not a competition. It is a life for each and every one of us to aspire to greatness. It is a life for each of us to fulfill our measure and become the incredible, powerful, and talented beings God intends us to become.

Happiness

doesn't come when we are constantly

looking to be accepted.

It comes when we REACH OUT

and are accepting of others.

CHAPTER 4

Can I

Sit Here?

In the back of my mind, I knew October

1st was approaching . . . . It was time

for me to decide if I would quit or if

I would continue to compete.

Throughout the 2003–2004 World Cup skeleton season, I didn't feel like I belonged. All I wanted was to be accepted by my teammates and coaches. I wanted to feel like I fit in, but quite honestly I felt like a piece of ham on a peanut butter and jelly sandwich. I felt like I got in the way. I didn't have any friends, and the team seemed to be doing just fine without me.

I was 5,000 miles from my husband, Janson, and very unhappy with my circumstances. Day after day the schedule was the same. I woke up, got dressed in my winter clothes in preparation for a day on the icy track, went to breakfast in the hotel restaurant, and once again ate by myself. My coach would tell us all what time we would be leaving for the track. So at the designated time, I placed my equipment in the van and maneuvered my way to the back row as my teammates loaded their gear. They would sit in front and we'd drive away. No one would ask how I was or what I planned to do that day. No one really cared.

Once we got to the track, we each would grab our sled, helmet, and gear out of the van and walk into the building called the "start house." This building has benches lined up against the walls for athletes to sit and prepare for training and competitions. The first few days of the season, I went up to groups of athletes who were talking and laughing and asked if I could sit by them. I wanted to talk, laugh, and be a part of them. I wanted to feel accepted in the environment I would be in day after day. Each time, the response was the same. The spot was taken, the bench was full, or they needed the space for someone or something else . . . like their shoes or helmet.

I would find an empty spot away from everyone else and hope that someone would sit next to me to talk or say hello. I felt so out of place and just wanted someone, *anyone*, to say hi. Once in a while, one of my teammates would sit next to me and we'd talk about the track, but the conversation never grew into anything else. I'd slide down the track a handful of times, desperately focused on my results. I wanted to be the fastest to gain the attention of my coaches. I wanted to beat my teammates so they would pay attention to me. I wanted to win a medal to gain the praise of others. I was so focused on winning that I lost track of how winning really happens. I never won a medal that season. My best World Cup finish the entire season was a ninth-place result on a track in Switzerland, and I was extremely frustrated. After training every day, I packed up my gear, loaded it back into the van, climbed into the back seat by myself, and waited to head back to the hotel.

I worked out by myself, prepared my equipment by myself, and did everything else alone. I would see my teammates and teammates from other nations talking, laughing, going to the store, or seeing the town together, and I longed for someone to ask me to join them. I began avoiding others in order to avoid the feeling of being left out. It was a lot easier to lock myself in my room and not know what was going on than to see and feel hurt by everything I was missing out on.

When we sat down at the dinner table, the chairs closest to me were always the last to be filled. Conversations would carry on, but I was never included in them. In fact, if anyone did say something to me, it was, "Cover your ears 'cause you're not gonna like this." I felt alone day after day and month after month. I would try to strike up conversations, but anyone I spoke to would act uninterested or completely ignore what I was saying. Sometimes I was even the brunt of others' jokes because I wouldn't swear, drink alcohol, or watch inappropriate movies. I really wanted to be accepted and comfortably interact with everyone, but it seemed that I had too much going against me. I wasn't happy. In fact, I was flat-out miserable.

I was so focused on me, myself, and I that I couldn't see past my thoughts of loneliness and despair. I was ready to quit just to get out of this miserable situation. I was ranked fourteenth in the world, third in the United States, and had a chance to move up, but I was stuck in a seriously gloomy state and I made myself believe that skeleton didn't matter to me anymore. In fact, the spring of 2004, I flew home from Europe (where I had been competing for the past few months), unloaded my equipment from the car, immediately shoved it into our outdoor shed, and forgot all about it.

✶ ✶ ✶ ✶ ✶ ✶ ✶ ✶

I moved on with my spring and summer. I was back with Janson and extremely happy to be home. I focused on my junior year of running track and field at Utah Valley University and dedicated myself to working toward graduation. I spent time with my family, coached a junior high track and field team, and honestly had no intention of going back to skeleton.

During the summer, skeleton athletes usually spend time managing and tuning up their equipment. Hours upon hours are spent fixing up and rebuilding a sled. Changes are made in the international rules, which requires making adjustments. New gear is purchased and polished. Training regimens are most intense throughout the summer, with athletes intent on returning to the sport in October in the best shape possible. An Olympic athlete might spend between three and ten hours a day working out and fine-tuning the skills needed to compete against the best athletes in the world.

Janson and I decided to enjoy our summer by traveling and spending time together. We visited Lake Powell in southern Utah, went to California to swim in the ocean, went camping in Idaho, and played coed softball three or four nights each week. In the meantime, my sled and equipment were still strapped tightly inside the custom suitcase that sat in the incredibly hot shed in our backyard.

In the back of my mind, I knew October 1st was approaching, which meant sliding would begin and that I would need to tell my coach I wasn't planning to come back. But I continued to push the thought away and instead would look forward to the next softball game or vacation. I was happy, and I didn't want to change that. But the clock kept ticking, as time tends to do, and soon it was three weeks until sliding and competitions would begin. U.S. Nationals were the first competitions of the year. Those races determine who will compete on World Cup. It was time for me to decide if I would quit or if I would continue to compete.

Janson and I spent countless hours talking this over, praying for guidance to make the right decision. I knew what my heart and mind felt. I did not want to put myself back in that environment. I was reminded of the misery and solitude that I felt day after day. It was very difficult to push my feelings aside and to really try to feel and know what I should do, but it soon became clear to me what needed to happen. As I read in Matthew 7:24–25, I knew that I needed a stronger foundation.

"Therefore whosoever HEARETH these sayings of mine,

and DOETH THEM, I will liken him unto a

wise man *which* **built his**

house upon a rock:

And the *rain descended,* and the *floods came,*

and the **winds blew,** and **beat upon that house;**

and it **FELL NOT:** For it was

founded upon a rock."

I had built my very unstable foundation and my whole outlook on how I would fit into a situation, a conversation, or a group of people.

I knew that I needed to change my attitude and step outside of myself. Janson and I decided that I would compete that season but only if some major changes took place.

First, I knew I wasn't where I needed to be spiritually and mentally. I needed to set goals for myself and stick to them.

Next, I made a resolution to be a friend. A wise leader gave us a great explanation of what it means to be a friend: "We are something less than a real friend if we leave a person the same way we find him [or her]. . . . Acts of a friend should result in self-improvement, better attitudes, self-reliance, comfort, consolation, self-respect, and better welfare. . . . Fear can deprive us of friendship. . . . It takes courage to be a real friend." I wanted to be a friend. I wanted to have the courage to look for others that felt left out or that were sitting by themselves and reach out to them. I realized that I was possibly to blame for many of my own feelings of insecurity, misery, and loneliness. We *always* have a choice. We have a choice to be alone, to think negatively, and to feel helpless and out of place in a situation, or we can think positively, look for opportunities to serve, and seek out those who might need a friend. An incredible poet, Ralph Waldo Emerson, was wise in saying, "The only way to have a friend is to be one."

I decided I would strive to look outward, searching for opportunities to serve and chances to gain a friend. I wanted to look for the best qualities in every person and every athlete, regardless of how they treated me. In the scriptures we are taught to love everyone, even those we don't get along with, or in some cases, are competing against. I wanted to implement Matthew 5:44 in my life:

"But I say unto you, *love your enemies*, **bless them** that curse you, DO GOOD TO THEM that hate you, and *pray for them* which despitefully use you, and persecute you."

I knew it wouldn't be easy, but it gave me hope that this season would be different. This season would be better.

Finally, I decided to truly let go of my need to cross the finish line first and my desire to beat the other athletes. I knew that I had been blessed with talents and abilities, and I realized that nothing in this life is ever really a competition against someone else. All we can ever give is our best. All we can ever do is learn, work, grow, and develop our talents the best we can. We have each been blessed with a different set of talents, so it is unfair to compare ourselves with one another. Whether you believe it or not, it is a fact that God has blessed every one of us with innumerable, unique talents. I decided that as long as I gave *my* best, and looked outside of myself, this season would be great regardless of my results.

I began to think positively and truly saw life differently. I let go of my need to succeed and prayed to our Father in Heaven that I would be

THE ONLY WAY TO HAVE

a friend

IS TO BE ONE.

—RALPH WALDO EMERSON

positive, happy, and reflect the light of Christ in any way that I could. I prayed to see others that might be in need of a friend and to have the courage to talk to them. I called my coach and told him I would be at Nationals in two short weeks. I began my rigorous workouts, unpacked my sled and equipment from our shed, and purchased a ticket to Lake Placid, New York. Janson spent the next two weeks fixing my equipment to be race-ready just in time for me to fly away.

* * * * * * * *

I arrived at the Olympic Training Center in Lake Placid and instantly remembered the feelings of insecurity and dread. I resolutely pushed them away, even though doing so meant I almost had to imagine myself as someone else. I had to imagine myself not as the person I thought I was, and not as the person I believed others pictured me to be, but as the person that I *wanted* to be.

I remember eating dinner that first night in the cafeteria and looking over to a table in the corner. In the past, I had often found myself sitting at that table alone, using my homework as an excuse to hide away from anyone that might notice me and make me feel embarrassed. Without delay, I turned away from the corner and looked around the room. I saw the groups I had once longed to be a part of. I recognized the conversations and the laughter that I had previously hoped to be involved in. I continued to look over these tables filled with athletes and coaches, and that's when it happened. I noticed a girl sitting at a table on the opposite end of the cafeteria. She was staring at the group that had originally caught my eye, and I could see her desire to be a part of the crowd. This girl seemed to be out of place and uncomfortable with where she was. As I approached her she looked around, wondering where I was going or if there was someone near her who I was going to sit by. I was nervous and wondered just what I would do next. *Maybe she just wants to sit by herself. Maybe I should just sit at the table next to her by myself,* I thought. Then another thought came. *Nope. It's time for a change, Noelle.*

"Can I sit here?" I asked.

"Sure," she replied with a smile. I learned that this girl was a development athlete competing in skiing aerials and this was her first time coming to Lake Placid. She didn't know anyone there and was pretty nervous. We talked and laughed. Over the next hour and a half, we learned about each other and became friends. Over the next three weeks of my stay in Lake Placid, our paths crossed nearly every day in the cafeteria. We would say hi, ask about each other's day, laugh, and share experiences. I continued to gather courage as I searched for others that were alone at the track, in the gym, or at mealtime and tried to make a friend. I knew that there were others who might be having a bad day and needed a glimpse of hope, even if all that meant was someone smiling and saying hi to them.

Race day arrived and I finished second at Nationals, which placed me on the World Cup team along with four men and two other women. We left the Olympic Training Center and flew to Europe. I continued to train hard and dedicated myself to my goals. Our first race was on a track in Winterberg, Germany. I had never been to this track before, which is a big disadvantage to any athlete, but I was happy and just looking forward to seeing what my best was.

Race day came and I surprised the world. I had the fastest times of the competition. I had won my first World Cup race, and my confidence soared. I continued to wear the yellow leader bib throughout the entire season as I won multiple races. I was ranked first in the world. At the

I decided that regardless of my results, as long as I gave my best and looked outside of myself, this season would be great.

end of the 2005 season, I became the first U.S. woman to ever win the Overall World Cup title in skeleton. The 2006 Olympics were just a year away, and I was number one in the world. It was absolutely incredible. I was truly on top of the world.

Even more meaningful, though, was that throughout the entire season, regardless of my results, I kept the goals I had made for myself. I read my scriptures and said my prayers morning and night. I stood firm in my beliefs and stayed positive. I made a continual effort to sit next to those who were alone and left my own feelings of loneliness and despair behind. I recognized that feeling accepted in any situation is a matter of attitude and courage. Happiness doesn't come when we are constantly looking to be accepted. It comes when we reach out and are accepting of others. I gave it my best and stopped comparing myself to other athletes and their talents. I learned the difference between observing others in an effort to learn and improve my own skills and comparing myself in a way that brought me down and made me feel inferior. I allowed myself to be happy with my best effort no matter what time the clock showed as I crossed the finish line.

My outlook, my attitude, and ultimately my results were completely altered in those three short weeks leading up to my competitions. Despite my fitness level not being where it should have been or my equipment being run down from the heat of our shed, I was ready to accept my best efforts and ready to accept others around me. I was willing and determined to do anything necessary to avoid the feelings of despair and loneliness.

When we don't feel accepted, we shouldn't seek for others to invite us along or hope that someone will notice us and include us in a conversation or activity. We need to leave behind our negative thoughts, self-pity, and feelings of loneliness. Step outside of your comfort zone and look for those who could use a smile or a friend. Have the courage to say hi. A simple phrase, "Can I sit here?" opened my eyes to countless opportunities to make new friends, meet interesting people, and partake of happiness in my life that I had previously missed out on. Take courage to meet new people and make new friends. Dare to be who you *want* to be.

It is

easier to

STAND
WITH
COURAGE

in the days to come if you

decide today who you are
and what you stand for.

CHAPTER 5

Dare to

Stand Alone

> I had decided a long time ago that I
> wouldn't let the vision and expectations
> of the world determine who I am
> or what I stand for.

I love being a girl!

I love the options for hairstyles and accessorizing every outfit. Some days I love frilling up and others I love drabbing down. I like to wear a skirt on Sunday and my baseball cap on Monday. I love my colorful high heels and my assortment of belts that can really "make an outfit."

I love the joys of womanhood. I love the natural care and concern that we as women have for others. I absolutely love being a mom, and I cherish the responsibility and blessing of having children. I am forever grateful to those around me who also serve as mothers to my children. As women, we are compassionate, giving, and loving. We also have a need and desire to be loved. Unfortunately, we can at times be blinded by the world's opinion of how this love and adoration is obtained.

* * * * * * * * *

Before my first Olympic appearance, I was invited to attend an incredibly comprehensive social event known as the Media Summit. This national event attracts every newspaper, magazine, television broadcast, charity foundation, and webcast with any interest in sports, health, or fitness. Athletes expected to do well in the Olympics received invitations to attend, and we were asked to bring a variety of clothes to wear throughout the event. They wanted workout clothes, "Sunday best," formal wear, competition gear and equipment, "going out" outfits, winter gear, and then basically anything else left in your closet after packing all of these items.

When I arrived in West Hollywood, I was greeted by a young man named Wes. He said he would be my escort throughout the Summit. We loaded my bags into a very nice black limousine and went directly to the infamous SmashBox Studios, known worldwide for its award-winning film and photo shoots. As we approached the building, we slowed to wait for multiple camera crews as they crossed through the streets carrying massive fuzzy microphones, tripods, camera cases, and props. The limo parked, and just as I paused

to take a deep breath and take in the hustle of everyone around me, Wes said, "All right, we're here. We have three minutes until your first appearance. This will be with *Parent Magazine* and should last four minutes. Then I will escort you upstairs for a nine-minute interview with *USA Today*. After that interview, you will have a twenty-minute photo shoot with NBC, and you'll have to change into your competition gear for that one. Once that is complete I'll fill you in on what's next." The next two days were filled minute by minute. I would enter a room, shake two or three hands and say hello to everyone, sit on a chair as a tech crew member attached a microphone to my shirt, and the camera would roll. I would answer any and all questions. Some were basic: "How did you get into this sport? Tell us about when you were hit by a bobsled. How do you expect to do in the Olympics? How is it being a mom and an Olympic athlete?" Others were a bit more out there: "What is the weirdest food you have ever tried? Which actress would you want to play you in a movie about your life? Can you sing *Jingle Bells* for us?" I would shake their hands once again and exit the room only to enter another one identical to it but with different faces.

I was changing my clothes, accessories, and shoes every fifteen to twenty minutes to match the style or atmosphere that the interview or photo shoot was going for. It was fun, but by the fourth, or maybe the twenty-fourth change, I was exhausted.

Near the end of the Media Summit, Wes explained to me that one of the biggest photo shoots was just ahead. There would be photographers from Getty Images, NBC, *Women's Health*, *Shape Magazine*, the Associated Press, and many others. Many photographers were asking the athletes to show off their bodies. They wanted to see the muscles and definition. They clapped and cheered as the athletes posed. I was rushed into my final interview before this photo shoot, and as soon as I came out of the interview and into the massive studio room filled with lights, backdrops, and props, three women grabbed my suitcases out of my hands, opened them up, and sprawled my clothes out across a table. They were discussing what I should wear for each part of the shoot. Another woman, Diane, grabbed my hand and rushed me off to what appeared to be a makeshift dressing room. Amidst the pandemonium of people running around, lights flashing, and people shouting, a black curtain hung from a pole to somewhat shield the person changing from everyone else's view. As I stepped behind this curtain, the three women came running in with my clothes and told me what to wear and when to put each outfit on.

"One minute!" I heard someone yell. Diane told me that I would be changing many times in the next fifteen minutes and that I needed to do it as quickly as possible. I'm obviously competitive, so I saw this as a challenge. I quickly dressed and rushed out. As soon as I exited I was told to sit in a chair and wave flags. "Two minutes to dress change!" Two minutes flew by as the cameras around me clicked away and suddenly I was back behind the curtain, changing into my winter coat and snow pants. "Thirty seconds!" the same man yelled. I ran out of the dressing room and the setting had already  changed. I was instructed to play in the snow shooting from a fake snow blower. "Two minutes!" he yelled once again. I played in the snow as the camera crew moved around me, taking photos and encouraging me to smile or pose with a "game face." The time ended and I ran back into the changing room. "One minute!" I quickly removed my winter gear and slipped into my Sunday best. The lighting had changed, and I was now doing portrait shots. All I really wanted right then was a mirror, because

I knew my hair was a disaster from changing my clothes so many times. "Twenty seconds until wardrobe change!" The camera clicked a dozen more times, and I ran back behind the curtain.

When I entered, Diane handed me a dress. "Three minutes, people!" The dress she handed me wasn't mine, and she could see my puzzled look. "All of the female athletes are getting their pictures taken in a red dress to support healthy hearts and healthy living. This will be absolutely gorgeous on you." I took the dress from her hands and saw what was on the hanger. The dress had spaghetti straps on the shoulders, it was very revealing in the front, and I doubted the length would have even come near my fingertips. I knew immediately that I could not wear it. *But it was for a good cause, right?* "Two minutes!" the man from behind the curtain yelled. *I mean, healthy hearts, come on. It's a good excuse to doll up! I've worked hard to get my body into this shape, and I want to show it off! Everyone is waiting for me. What am I going to say? I'd be the only athlete that didn't wear it!*

When it came down to it, though, wearing the dress or not was a very easy decision for me to make. I had decided a long time ago that I wouldn't let the vision and expectations of the world determine who I am or what I stand for. What I wear is one symbol of who I am and how I feel about myself. I handed the dress back to Diane and told her, "I want to be modest. It's just who I am, and I am sorry but I can't wear this." I expected her to roll her eyes and try to convince me to wear it, but she surprised me.

"Oh, sweetie, I'm a good Christian girl and completely understand and respect your beliefs. Let's find you something else to wear." I was shocked and elated by her understanding and support of my decision.

* * * * * * * * *

The experience reminded me of a quote from a favorite author: "As we go about living from day to day, it is almost inevitable that our faith will be challenged. We may at times find ourselves surrounded by others and yet standing in the minority or even standing alone concerning what is acceptable and what is not. Do we have the moral courage to stand firm for our beliefs, even if by so doing we must stand alone?" He has also stated, "You be the one to make a stand for right, even if you stand alone. Have the moral courage to be a light for others to follow. There is no friendship more valuable than your own clear conscience, your own moral cleanliness—and what a glorious feeling it is to know that you stand in your appointed place clean and with the confidence that you are worthy to do so."

That brief moment in the dressing room had been a test of my beliefs. I felt validated realizing I had been able and willing to stand alone, and it gave me strength. It has since given me increased courage to walk away from situations I did not feel comfortable in or change a conversation I did not feel was appropriate. Find your courage, and dare to stand alone for what you believe in.

Diane dug deep in a box of clothes and found a dress that definitely wasn't very flattering, but it was modest. I can still find pictures of myself wearing that dress on the internet, and I cringe at the style every time I see it. But it reminds me of something more. What I wear doesn't define who I am. I know who I am and what I stand for regardless of what the world does or what people say or think around me. I don't need or want attention from showing off my body. It is sacred to me.

Four years later I attended the same Media Summit, held in the same location. As I made my rounds through interviews and photo shoots, I came to a setting similar to the one I remembered. I entered a very large

You be the one to make a stand for right, even if you stand alone. Have the moral courage to be a light for others to follow. There is no friendship more valuable than your own clear conscience, your own moral cleanliness—and what a glorious feeling it is to know that you stand in your appointed place clean and with the confidence that you are worthy to do so.

—THOMAS S. MONSON

room with bright lights, shouting, and camera crews everywhere. As I stepped in the door a woman took my hand and gave me a big hug. It was Diane. "I remember you! You're that good Christian girl. We don't have any immodest clothing for you to wear this time." It brought a smile to my face not only because I had stood up for my beliefs but also because I had left a positive impression on someone else.

* * * * * * * *

As my husband, kids, and I have traveled for my competitions, we have had numerous opportunities to see marvels in countries across the world. In February of 2014, just a few days before the Opening Ceremonies of the Olympic Winter Games in Sochi, Russia, we decided to spend the day at the Black Sea, just a few miles from where we were staying. Locals were setting up their shops on the beach walkway. Others were playing volleyball and enjoying the unusually warm weather for February. Our kids found sticks and drew designs in the sand. Just then a wave crashed on the beach, and the attention of our kids was drawn from the sand to the water. They ran across the open beach, threw their shoes on the ground, rolled up their pants, and stepped onto the wet sand. They waited for the next wave to crash, and as it did they would squeal and run away to avoid getting wet. As they gathered small rocks and began to throw the pebbles into the salty sea, my six-year-old daughter inquired, "Is this the ocean?"

"No," I replied. "It's the Black Sea."

"Why is it called the Black Sea? That's silly. It isn't black. It's blue!"

Her questions made me imagine being a sailor and looking for the "Black Sea." I would sail into its waters, see that it was actually blue, and leave! It really is silly, as my daughter says, to pretend to be something

you aren't. Sometimes we might have a tendency to act a certain way, talk negatively about others, use foul language, or even wear certain clothes to try to fit in or draw attention to ourselves, but it is a very dangerous line to walk. If we're not careful, we might portray ourselves in a way that will attract the wrong "sailors" to our sea of friendships and relationships.

Remember who you are and what you stand for. Remember to take courage. It is easy and probably even natural to be afraid. Joshua 1:9 reminds us that we are never alone:

"HAVE NOT I COMMANDED THEE?

Be strong and of a good courage;

be not afraid, **neither be thou dismayed:**

FOR THE LORD THY GOD IS WITH THEE

whithersoever thou goest."

I love it. I want to shout it out loud. "Be strong and of a good courage; be not afraid!" It isn't always easy to be the only one standing up for something you believe in. But I can promise you that it is much easier to stand with courage in the days to come if you decide now, today, in *this* moment, who you are and what you stand for. I love to make lists. I challenge you to make a list of what you want to improve on in your life. Maybe an area where you lack courage or an area that weighs you down because you know you should be standing a little taller and setting a better example. Let's move forward together and improve a little each day. I am grateful to be a daughter, a sister, a woman, and a mom. I love being a girl. I especially love being a girl that knows who she is and what she stands for.

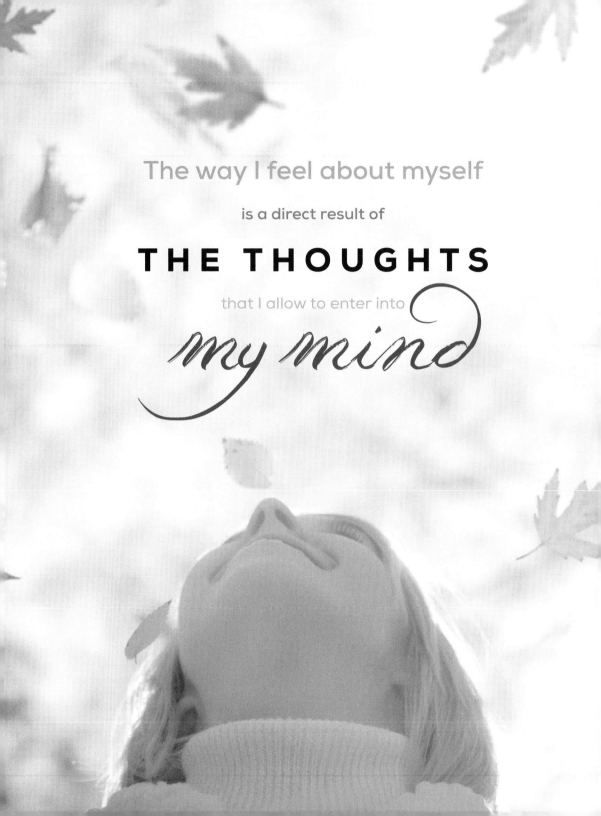

The way I feel about myself

is a direct result of

THE THOUGHTS

that I allow to enter into

my mind

CHAPTER 6

A Model

of Perfection

The "world" tried to tell me that

I was not good enough. . . .

And I believed it for a moment.

***

The summer before the 2010 Winter Olympic Games, I was invited to model the Ralph Lauren clothing the athletes would wear throughout the Olympics. The photos would be used for campaign ads promoting this worldwide event. I was extremely excited to have been picked as one of nine athletes to be photographed, and my self-esteem and confidence soared. Only two other female athletes had been asked to participate. The photo shoot took place in a large studio complex in New York City, where some of the top photographers, lighting specialists, and hair and makeup artists in the world were waiting for us to arrive. I showed up wide-eyed and elated to have been chosen as a model. The atmosphere was energetic, with crews running around preparing for the long day ahead. The crew looked very classy and chic. Everyone working around us was dressed to impress.

When you participate in a photo shoot or a major interview for television, they usually ask that you show up without any makeup on and your hair undone because they prefer to do it for you. As I waited for my turn to get "dolled up," I talked with the other athletes about their training programs and our upcoming seasons, which were less than a month away. We all seemed to be in decent shape after a summer of rigorous workouts and exercise programs, and we were excited to compete and see how our training would pay off. During our conversation, a woman named Joan, in charge of wardrobe, approached me. She asked me to follow her to a changing room, and with a brisk walk, we made our way to the opposite end of the room, where a temporary dressing room had been built in the corner. She handed me a stack of clothes to try on. "Try these on and then come out. We will have our seamstress alter your clothes and take them in where needed so they fit just right." As Joan shut the curtain, I held up the first pair of pants and immediately knew they would not fit. They were a size four. I was a size ten. These definitely would not need to be taken in. I immediately came out, very embarrassed and not sure what to do but knowing I couldn't possibly even try to fit into these clothes. I walked around the room looking for the woman that had handed me these clothes and finally found her at a clothing rack sifting through the options for every athlete.

"Excuse me," I said as she pulled her glasses down from her eyes and let them rest at the tip of her nose.

Joan glanced over the rim of her glasses. "Yes?"

"These clothes you gave me are too small. Can I get larger sizes?"

She let out a heavy sigh and replied, "Well, what size do you need?"

When I told her I needed a size ten, she shook her head quickly and said, "No, no. You aren't a ten, you're smaller than that. Come on, let's go see what we have."

As I walked with her around the room to another clothing rack I remember feeling very large and self-conscious. I wished I hadn't eaten such a big breakfast. I wanted to be so much smaller than I was. At a clothing rack she quickly pushed aside a row of hangers and grabbed a pair of pants. "You look like a size six. These are a size seven and I'm sure they will fit. They are the largest size we have. Now hurry and try them on so we can get you into hair and makeup." I took them, knowing once again they would be too small but hoping she was right. Maybe it would be my day and these clothes would run big.

I went into the dressing room and closed the curtain behind me. I began to dress in the new clothing but soon found myself wanting to sneak out of the door and pretend I wasn't there. The pants were supposed to fit loosely, and they were extremely tight. I couldn't even button them at the top. I wanted to cry. The shirt was extremely tight and showed every detail and flaw of my body. I couldn't get myself to leave the dressing room with the way that the clothes fit, so I just stood there wondering what to do. Just as I was about to undress and tell Joan that it simply wasn't going to work, I heard her voice as the curtain flew open. "Are you done in there?" Her reaction and body language upon seeing me confirmed my own thoughts and self-conscious beliefs. She shook her head, placed one hand on her very thin hip, and brought her other hand to her chin as though she would rest her head upon it. "This just won't do." She took a step out of the room, waved her hand in the air, and with a snap of her fingers shouted out a name. "Rebecca!" She waved her hand frantically, gesturing to Rebecca to come quickly to her aid. The woman stood at her side with a tape measure around her neck and a handful of seamstress tools in a handy belt around her small waist. They began pulling at my shirt and pants, demanding that I turn or lift my arms. Joan spoke very quickly, pointing to me and different parts of my body, shaking her head and waving her hands in the air. "I don't know what you can do with this, Rebecca, but I know you're a miracle worker. Come get me once Noelle is dressed appropriately." Without speaking to me, Rebecca began measuring my body, marking the clothing with a pencil, and motioning for me to turn. I was extremely relieved once she had finished and told me I could change back into my own clothes. I exited the changing room and handed her the clothes to be drastically altered. I felt horrible about myself.

Now, fully aware of my body shape and flaws, I began to wonder how the other athletes were doing. As I looked around the room, I realized that I was definitely the largest female athlete in the group. Figure skaters and cross country skiers are generally very petite athletes. The others were still laughing and talking, and they looked amazing. They had just finished getting their hair and makeup done. Their clothes fit just right, and another seamstress was actually taking in their clothing because it was too big on them.

I quickly went in to get my hair and makeup done, and after being told that my hair was extremely dry and unmanageable and that my skin needed moisturizer and care, I came out feeling like a penguin at a flamingo exhibit. That day was one of the absolute longest days of my life. I watched as the crews invited each athlete to stand in front of the lights, holding props and changing outfits. The camera flashed time and time again. The director was pleased and the photographer was very happy with the shots he was capturing. Finally, they asked me to take my place up front. I honestly felt like they asked me to stand there because they had to. "Turn to your side and look at me," the photographer would say. "Okay, there we go." The lights would flash, he would pause a moment and look at the images on his camera screen. "No. That's not going to work. Turn your body away and keep your chin up." Again, the lights would flash, again he would look at the images, and again he'd stop and say, "No, no. Let's see. Hair and makeup! Her hair isn't working. Can you fix it? Do something else with it." Those working on hair and makeup immediately showed up at my side and curled, applied, touched up, and rearranged my look. I felt embarrassed, self-conscious, awkward, and miserable.

"We're out of time. That will have to do," the director stated impatiently. "We'll take care of the rest in post." That meant whatever flaws they thought I had they would eliminate in editing. As if I could have felt any worse, he had just made me feel even smaller. The cameras continued to capture images and the lights continued to flash.

A few weeks went by and I received an email with one image from the photo shoot that they were going to use in their campaign. I opened the attachment, anxiously wondering which image they had decided to use. They had taken one image of each of the athletes and edited everyone together into one scene. I stared at the faces one by one, very discouraged when I saw that they had decided not to use me in their media efforts. I counted how many athletes they had decided to use and was confused when I counted nine athletes—the same amount of athletes that had been there the day of the photo shoot. I looked over the faces again and did a double-take. There was a face that I almost recognized, but I had to stare a moment longer to really comprehend that the person I was looking at was me! The body was much, much smaller than my own. The nose and cheekbones on this person had been altered and thinned out. Where once had been freckles and wrinkles I now saw only smooth and flawless skin. This face was "without imperfection." This person that I stared at in disbelief was not me. Aside from a glimmer of myself in the eyes, this person in the picture in front of me was a fake.

When my husband returned from work that night I asked him what he thought about the image they had decided to use. He was disappointed that they hadn't used me in their campaign. I also sent the image to my parents and sister, none of whom recognized that I was in the photo until I pointed to the helmet the person in the ad was holding to prove that it was, in fact, me.

* * * * * * * *

The "world" tried to tell me that I was not good enough. They told me I was too big, my hair was unmanageable, my skin was flawed, and that I did not fit in. And I believed it for a moment. It was a moment of despair, guilt, negativity, and misery. I wanted to be someone else. I wished my body looked how they wanted it to look. It was clear that I was not what they wanted.

A wonderful poem helps remind me how we are actually defined:

Not

You are not your age,
Nor the size of clothes you wear,
You are not a weight,
Or the color of your hair.
You are not your name,
Or the dimples in your cheeks,
You are all the books you read,
And all the words you speak,
You are your croaky morning voice,
And the smiles you try to hide,
You're the sweetness in your laughter,
And every tear you've cried,
You're the songs you sing so loudly,
When you know you're all alone,
You're the places that you've been to,
And the one that you call home,
You're the things that you believe in,
And the people that you love,
You're the photos in your bedroom,
And the future you dream of,
You're made of so much beauty,
But it seems that you forgot,
When you decided that you were defined,
By all the things you're not.

–Erin Hanson

As I stared at the image in front of me and understood what "the world" views as perfection and beauty, I was upset, saddened, but almost relieved. I was upset to know that the images we see every single day on television, the internet, and in magazines are contorted and end up making us feel that we are not enough. These false images cloud our minds with negative thoughts and unrealistic expectations of ourselves. I was saddened that girls everywhere lose track of themselves, their talents, and their beauty in an effort to become this false image that has been created through editing. I was in decent shape, as I had spent many hours in the gym training for Olympic competition, and I still wasn't even close to what they wanted me to be. Where would that place non-Olympians? Is this really the view and image we have all come to accept? I was relieved when I realized that I would never look like this person in the picture but that quite frankly, I didn't want to. The energy, time, money, surgeries, and lack of meals that would be required to make me look like that would never appeal to me for any amount of attention that "the world" would give me. My self-worth is priceless regardless of my weight, unmanageable hair, large shoe size, or freckles on my face. The way I feel about myself is a direct result of the thoughts that I allow to enter into my mind. It doesn't depend on who walks by me or what is said to me. My self-worth—as well as the way I view others in the world—is a choice I make in my own mind and within my own thoughts. If someone tells me that I am not beautiful, I have a choice to accept it or to let it go, knowing that ultimately how I feel about myself is all that matters.

A quote I have reminded myself of through competitions and daily living is one from Eleanor Roosevelt: "No one can make you feel inferior without your consent."

As I have observed the strength, skill, and beauty of the athletes

No one
can make you feel
INFERIOR
without your consent.

—Eleanor Roosevelt

I have had to compete against, it has been a challenge to stay away from the comparison trap. It is so easy to compare myself to them in every way, which could easily result in negative thoughts and doubts about my own skills and abilities. I have had to teach myself to be aware of my thoughts in order to eliminate these destructive patterns and habits. Proverbs 23:7 reminds us of the importance of the thoughts we entertain about ourselves:

"FOR AS HE THINKETH **in his** *heart,* SO IS HE."

I have been able to achieve the greatest of success because of what I choose to think and believe about myself. The person that I saw in the image from the photo shoot was a model of perfection in the eyes of the world. But I know that God made me the way that I am and He is a perfect being. I have divine attributes and potential. I am not the fake person in the photograph or any other person except me. Never allow the world's ideal image for you to diminish who you really are or what you were meant to offer.

Life is full of possibilities. There are people on this earth that only you can reach out to. There are people in this life that only you, the way you are, can serve, influence, or help. We have each been blessed with beautiful bodies that come in every shape, size, color, and detail. Each of us has been sent to this earth for a purpose. God loves us all and created us as we are with the hope that we would love ourselves and believe in our beauty and potential.

CHAPTER 7

A Well-Balanced Life

If we place too much emphasis on any one aspect of our lives, it can become difficult, if not impossible, to balance and grow.

How do you do it all?" has to be one of the most common questions I am asked. As a mom, an Olympic athlete, a business owner, an active member of my church, and all the other roles we are often asked to fill, it all comes down to exercise. I bet you didn't see that one coming, did you? It takes all kinds of exercise. Just as my body needs exercise and balance to stay healthy, my spiritual, mental, and social sides of life must be regularly exercised and balanced as well.

* * * * * * * *

There was a point in our marriage when my husband and I were playing coed softball four or five nights a week. We loved softball and really enjoyed the time we were able to spend together socializing with our teammates. Our daughter, Lacee, was a year old, and most nights one of our parents or siblings would come to watch the game and care for her.

We would travel all over the state to participate in tournaments. Any time someone would call us to play, we would drop everything to join, regardless of weather conditions or the distance we would need to drive. We bought new bats, cleats, and gloves and justified our purchases by pointing out that softball provided good quality time together.

In the meantime, the house was constantly a disaster, dishes piled up in the sink, and laundry heaps were strewn everywhere. We would get invited to a neighborhood barbecue or asked to attend a piano recital for a nephew or niece and our reply was always the same. "We have a game and won't be able to make it." Mail piled up on the countertops, church activities were missed, and the books we had intentions to read collected a thick layer of dust.

At one point we realized our grass hadn't been mowed in eight weeks. It was over a foot long. We complimented ourselves on how green it was, but we knew that the yard needed some serious attention. The grass sprawled past the sidewalk and grew vigorously throughout the flower beds.

We didn't have time for anything except softball. I would wake up, take care of Lacee, run errands, put her down for a nap, do my skeleton workouts in my basement (with the baby monitor nearby), get Lacee ready, and take off out the door for another game. Janson would be at work all day and drive straight to the softball field. We would meet up, play for a couple of hours, go home, clean ourselves up, get ready for bed, and do it all again the next day. We were stressed, overwhelmed, and our lives were simply in disarray.

Our grass continued to grow. One day, as I was quickly packing up a backpack to take to the softball game that evening, I noticed a spot of grass in our backyard that had died. I figured we needed to water it more and rushed out the door. I forgot about that patch of grass for about a week until I happened to glance out the window just before another game. The brown patch of grass had doubled in size. As I ran out the door to meet Janson, I called him and mentioned that the water must not be hitting that spot of grass. A few days later, after another game, Janson adjusted the sprinklers and we forgot about it, figuring it was taken care of.

The following weekend we finally had a day away from the mounds and dirt and determined it was time to work on the yard. We could barely mow through one row of grass in the front yard before we had to empty the fully loaded bag of clippings. As we began to mow, we discovered something that we hadn't been able to see beneath the top of the nice, foot-long, dark green grass. After trimming the grass down to a normal length we could see that it was infested with slugs, bugs, and worms. It was disgusting. As I walked through it, the slugs stuck to my shoes and flicked up onto the back of my calves. I was so repulsed that I actually had to stop and make Janson mow the rest by himself.

Once we turned our attention to the backyard, we were shocked to see that the dead patch of grass had taken over a fourth of our yard. At first I was just happy that the dead patch meant really short grass without any slugs or bugs on it. Janson reached down to feel the grass, and as he pulled on it lightly the entire section came easily up from the ground.

We have to forego some

good

things

in order to

choose others

that are better or

—DALLIN H. OAKS

Only a pile of dirt was left in its place. We later learned that the little white worms we had seen throughout the grass in the front yard were also all over the backyard, but they had made their way into the dirt, eaten the roots of our grass, and killed it. We had a specialist come over to assess what we should do to save our yard, but he said that nothing could be done. It was too late. The worms had infested our entire yard. He walked over to the grass that we thought was healthy and could be saved. When he bent down and gave a little tug, the entire handful of grass easily pulled out of the ground just as the brown section had done before. Grubs had eaten our grass roots. The roots became shallow and were unable to take in the nutrients needed to sustain life. The only option we had was to tear out all of the grub-infested grass in our yard and pay to have new grass put in its place. The financial burden, time constraint, and worry over all of our unfulfilled responsibilities tipped us over the top.

✳ ✳ ✳ ✳ ✳ ✳ ✳ ✳

We officially realized that we had lost control of our lives. Just as the grub had eaten the roots of the grass and made it impossible to receive all of the nutrients needed to grow, we had unintentionally cut off our supply of nutrients for living and growth. As a favorite quote says, "We have to forego some good things in order to choose others that are better or best." This wisdom has become a mantra of mine and has helped me to make daily decisions that have ultimately brought balance, strength, peace, and freedom to my life.

If we place too much emphasis on any one aspect of our lives, it can become difficult, if not impossible, to balance and grow. We will lose the nutrients that come from all the other valuable realms of life. This can apply to school or work when we focus too much on one subject or job and then feel overwhelmed by every other subject that needs attention and time. Relationships also need a healthy balance. A strong and healthy relationship is one in which each wants the best for the other and encourages growth and development. Spending every minute together can ultimately inhibit each person's ability to learn, nurture skills, and develop talents.

It was good to play softball with my husband every night. It would have been better to play once or twice each week. And we learned it was best to ensure that our spiritual and mental well-beings were equally nourished as we made time for a variety of other activities in our lives.

Without balance in my life, I never would have been able to find the success that I have found as a student, friend, athlete, wife, or mom. I would have never been able to prevail above the overwhelming feelings of stress, discouragement, and insufficiency that can surround us when we are pressed for time.

Following the incident with the grass, we made some changes in our lives. We originally felt overwhelmed and discouraged, feeling like there was too much to be done and not enough time to do it. But we tried to heed counsel we'd been taught all our lives: Anything we do should be done in wisdom and order; there's no need to run faster than you're capable of running.

There was wisdom in simplifying our lives. Order in every aspect of our well-being was required. It was difficult to do, because we loved playing softball and the time we were able to spend together, but we chose to limit our playing time to once a week. We then spent time organizing every aspect of our lives. Every Sunday, I took time to map out my week on a giant office calendar. I would write down specific goals and items that needed my attention. I wrote down anything and everything pressing on my mind and scheduled time for these things on the calendar. Then each night I would look at my list for the next day and adjust my schedule when necessary.

As an athlete I have learned the detriment of placing unrealistic expectations on myself. I have to push myself to my limit, but not beyond. That it is when injury and setbacks occur. I have to allow time for rest and recovery. Unrealistic expectations are a great way to set ourselves up for disappointment and despair.

Mentally, I needed a little time for myself as well. I literally had to schedule time to *think*, even if it was just a few minutes sitting on the new, slug- and grub-free grass in our backyard and looking up at the stars or shutting the door to my closet and closing my eyes to have a moment to think about my life. We all need some moments of peace and reflection in our lives. We all need some time to internalize life around us and our place in this world. The times in my life when I have mentally or emotionally been at my limit, my constant place of refuge has been upon my knees. Our physical, emotional, and spiritual well-beings are intertwined. As we exercise each of these, the others gain strength as well.

I receive spiritual strength from reading the scriptures and praying daily. So I would schedule on my calendar fifteen minutes every morning after I woke up and every night before bed to exercise spiritually. I knew I would need to be physically rested in order to have the energy to rise a little earlier each day, which meant I set a goal to go to bed at a reasonable time each night. I wanted to find peace and harmony in my life. I recognized that the movies I watched, the music I listened to, and the conversations I had directly impacted my spirituality, so I exercised good choices in those areas as well.

In assessing my life after the grub attack on our yard, I realized I wanted to improve my emotional health and fitness as well. With the free time that I gained throughout the week, I was able to focus on organizing our home. It is amazing how our moods are easily swayed when our home is disorganized and cluttered. There was a recognizable serenity in our home as it became manageable once again. On my calendar I scheduled goals to clean out one room at a time. I wanted to feel the peace that can come from cleanliness and order. Day by day, I felt a little more accomplished and relieved by all of the things I was able to do now that my schedule had opened up. As I began to clean out our much-dreaded basement space, I came across my old photography developing equipment from a hobby I had once been passionate about. As I sifted through these items my passion was lit once again. I wanted to expand my knowledge in the area and soon enrolled in a college photography course. I am continuing to explore

My Goals This Month

Physical
* Workout 3 times each week
* Train outside of my comfort zone

Nutrition
* Eat in moderation
* Eat to make the most of my workouts
* Drink at least 10 glasses of water each day

Mental
* Take 10 minutes each day to "think" or plan next day
* Learn something new each day
* Visualize track and sliding atmosphere to be prepared and know where I want to go

Spiritual
* Say prayers and read scriptures morning and night
* Increase faith
* Fulfill church responsibilities

Social
* Go out of my way to make a new friend
* Be a better neighbor

I love to make lists of what I need to do and what I want to improve in my life. Setting small goals and organizing my life has not only allowed me to improve my talents, but it has also freed up time in my day to enjoy life and not just endure it.

new talents, hobbies, and experiences. Participating in these things has also strengthened my social well-being as well as I work with peers and make new friends.

Exercising my mind has given me self-confidence and a sense of achievement. It has strengthened me emotionally as I have found balance and continued to grow. We are granted learning opportunities every day. We are capable of exercising our spirits, minds, and bodies but it requires effort. It requires self-discipline. Exercising our lives requires us to make healthy choices every day.

Finally, as I felt the power that had come from organizing my life spiritually, mentally and socially, I knew that I had to place emphasis on my physical well-being. My dream of becoming an Olympic athlete was still vivid and strong, but once I had a baby, my priorities had changed. I couldn't imagine how I could put in all of the hours required to train and still have time for my family and everything else in my life. I spoke with my strength and conditioning coach and explained my situation. We determined that three days a week for three hours a day should be sufficient for me to reach my goals and maintain sanity in every other aspect of my life. He agreed that quality workouts versus quantity would be the key to my success. He understood and recognized the importance of taking time off for recovery and rest. We created a workout plan to support my goals. There were many days when the weights seemed too heavy and I didn't feel that I had the strength to go on. There were mornings when I just didn't want to train. Many times, my muscles would ache and my body was sore to the point that lifting the milk from the fridge was extremely demanding. But as I have witnessed so many times in my life, it is those small and simple things, like completing one more rep in a workout, studying five more minutes for a test, or saying no to something that you know you shouldn't do, that make the greatest impacts on our lives.

Alongside my workouts, nutrition is definitely one of the greatest mental battles I have ever had to face. It takes daily effort. There are constant decisions to be made. When I don't make healthy choices with my nutrition, I am very hard on myself. I feel guilty and discouraged. It becomes more difficult to get through my workouts and every other task that I need to accomplish. Eating poorly makes it hard to focus during daily activities like work or school. It diminishes our ability to think rationally and allows negative thoughts and feelings to flow freely through our minds. Ultimately, if our nutrition is not managed, we will fall victim to our own insecurities and guilt over our lack of control. Remember that there are always good, better, and best nutritional options.

Each of these aspects of our well-being—spiritual, mental, social, emotional, and physical—is irrefutably tied together. When one area falters and lacks our attention and effort, the others will ultimately be hindered.

* * * * * * * * *

We learned an important lesson the day we decided to mow our grass. We learned that just as the grass needed strong roots and many nutrients to grow, so did we. In life we always have the option to choose something good, better, or best. Our lives are greatly blessed when we purposefully analyze our choices and identify the areas that need improvements.

I could not have won an Olympic medal if I did not strive to maintain balance in my life. As I stood at the starting line at the Olympic Games, I knew I had prepared in every way for that moment. I felt at peace in my mind and heart. Spiritually, I was prepared through daily study and continued to move forward with positivity and faith. Mentally, I had studied out every aspect of every curve until I was confident in what I needed to do. Physically, I had taken care of my body and given all that I could each and every day that I trained. I was prepared for that race because I had made a diligent effort to exercise each aspect of my well-being. We each can feel relief, strength, peace, and growth as we focus on building our own stable, balanced foundations for life.

STAND TALL,

keep your head high

AND HAVE

faith.

CHAPTER 8

One Foot
in Front of
the Other

This was my final race and I wanted to go out on top of the world, but I couldn't figure out how to let go of the expectations and pressures that I felt.

am an Olympian! I repeated it over and over in my mind. The thousands upon thousands of hours had *finally* paid off. I couldn't believe that it was real. *I really am an Olympian!* I would have the opportunity to represent my country, the United States of America, at the 2010 Olympic Winter Games in Vancouver, Canada. My whole life I had wondered if this moment would ever be real.

There were two World Cup races left in the season for the bobsled and skeleton, but this was the final race that would solidify an Olympic berth. The race was held in St. Moritz, Switzerland. I had been on the road away from my husband and eighteen-month baby girl for the better part of ten months, and I could finally see the light at the end of the tunnel. I finished that final qualifying race in eighth place. To be honest, it was a fairly disappointing race and a discouraging year in general. In sports, you train and compete your whole life with the mindset that somehow it will eventually pay off. You want a medal, a trophy, applause, or recognition of some sort that validates all of your painstaking effort. I had been ranked first in the world before the previous Olympics, and then due to unforeseeable circumstances my course was altered. Ever since that moment all I wanted was a taste of that success.

After I had my daughter, I saw competition—and life—differently. I wanted to achieve *my* dream so that one day she would know *her* dreams could come true, too. I wasn't competing just for my own gratification and pride anymore. It was very difficult, however; I was no longer leaving only my husband behind when I left for competitions. The sacrifice became so much more once my daughter was born. My heart ached during the weeks and days that led up to my departures. I used to look forward to competing and seeing what I could do or who I could beat—now I just wanted to get through it. I would often turn to some trusted advice: "It was meant to be that life would be a challenge. To suffer some anxiety, some depression, some disappointment, even some failure is normal. . . . If [you] have a good, miserable day once in a while, or several in a row, . . . stand steady and face them. Things will straighten out. There is great purpose in our struggle in life."

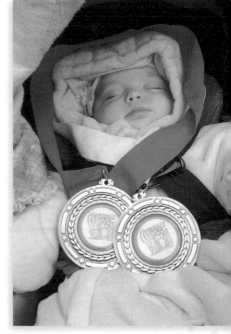

I knew I had to stand steady and face the difficult days. I knew that things would straighten out. I had a purpose. My goal was clear. More than anything, I wanted to reach my Olympic dream so that one day, when my daughter was older and struggling with a goal

THERE IS GREAT PURPOSE
IN OUR STRUGGLE

IN *life.*

—BOYD K. PACKER

in her life, I could turn to her and say, "I get it. I know it's hard and you want to give up. I've had hard days too and understand. I know there are days when you think that you can't go on. I know it seems easier to just quit, but you can make it. Just think about today and take it one step at a time. One hour at a time. I promise you those little things you do each day add up, and they will bring big results. Don't give in to those doubts, fears, and worries that so easily slip into your mind. Take a deep breath. Don't give up on yourself. You are loved. I know you are strong enough to get through this. You are beautiful, talented, and capable of greatness. Know that I'll always be here for you. Always. Keep your head high and you'll be there soon."

As I ponder those things I want my daughter to know, and every young woman to know, I can't help but draw an analogy between this and the love of our Savior. I can't help but think about all those times in my life when I was too weak, literally or figuratively, to stand. When my heart was broken and the sadness felt as though it would shoot from my fingertips and toes. When I sobbed and pled desperately on my knees at the foot of my bed for a glimmer of peace and comfort. When I think about those times when I felt stuck and unable to go on, I can only imagine our Savior saying, "I get it. I know it's hard and you want to give up. I've had hard days too, and I understand. I know there are days when you think that you can't go on. I know it seems easier to just quit, but you can make it. Just think about today and take it one step at a time. One hour at a time. I promise you those little things you do each day add up, and they will bring big results. Don't give in to those doubts, fears, and worries that so easily slip into your mind. Take a deep breath. Don't give up on yourself. You are loved. I know you are strong enough to get through this. You are beautiful, talented, and capable of greatness. Know that I'll always

be here for you. Always. Keep your head high and you'll be there soon."
I know the Savior lives. He knows you. He loves you.

* * * * * * * * *

As had been the norm for the past two years, at this World Cup race
I was competing with my mind and body but my heart was thousands of
miles away with my family. I longed for them. I wanted to hold my girl.
I missed her first steps, her first words, and her first birthday. It was extremely painful to be away from her.

After finishing eighth that day in the final World Cup competition, I
was disappointed with the results of the season but extremely relieved
and elated that my dream of becoming an Olympian had come true.
I wanted to let go of the past. I wanted to let go of the pain and disappointment of missing out on the 2006 Olympics because of the accident.
I wanted to let go of my need to win and my fear of failure. I wanted to
let go of the sadness wound so tightly in my chest over leaving my family.
I wanted to be free. I wanted to find my passion and my drive to compete
one last time. This was it. I was done. I had one race left, the Olympic
Games, and then Janson and I could mark this dream fulfilled and move
on with our lives.

That night as the team was announced and athletes and coaches cel-
ebrated, I began to prepare mentally for what was to come. I could feel
the pressure that I was putting on myself to do well in order to justify the
sacrifices I was making in leaving my family. I could feel the pressure of
being the top-ranked athlete in the United States, and the expectations
of my coaches were constantly racing through my mind. I imagined myself standing at the starting line in Vancouver. I pictured the snow falling
and the crowd cheering. I could see the icy track in front of me and each

curve that I would need to navigate. I could see each of my top competitors, and I began to compare myself with them. I'm not the fastest sprinter and I knew the other girls would beat me at the top of the track, which immediately brought doubts into my mind. I saw the camera crews, journalists, press conferences, and expectations of the world now on my shoulders. I could see every detail of the atmosphere and competition . . . and my heart began to race. My palms were clammy. Fear shot throughout my body. I wanted so desperately to do well. This was my final race and I wanted to go out on top of the world, but I couldn't figure out how to let go of the expectations and pressures that I felt.

I was sitting on a couch in a hotel lobby, 5,420 miles and three weeks from my Olympic competition, and I was already having a nervous breakdown. *Oh great. This is just how I expected it to end.* My mom had always taught me to expect the worst and hope for the best, but I don't think this was quite what she had in mind. How was I going to compete at my best and reach my potential while overwhelmed with thoughts of fear, worry, and panic?

As I looked around the room at the celebratory ambiance, I noticed one of the bobsled coaches and five-time Olympian, Brian Shimer,

The view from the top of the Vancouver Olympic Site was one that I had pictured in my mind a thousand times before. But I could have never dreamed the feelings of elation and joy I felt as I stood at the top of the track and looked down toward the finish line a mile below.

away from all the rest and sitting in a corner by himself. He seemed to be taking in the evening and reminiscing on times past. In this moment when I should have been feeling happy and light, I felt scared and weighed down. I really needed someone to talk to. I walked through the crowd, faking a smile and congratulating those around me as they did the same to me. Brian saw me approaching and motioned for me to take a seat.

I asked him question after question about what to expect at the Olympics. He had been there multiple times, and I wanted to know everything. From past experience, I knew that the more I could learn, the more prepared I would be and the less fear I would feel. After forty minutes of soaking in every detail and bit of advice he shared, I asked him, "Okay. But how do you give it your absolute best in the moment that the green light goes off? The whole world is watching! What do you eat? How much do you lift the week of the competition? How do you stay focused? There are going to be so many people and cameras everywhere. How do you compete when there is so much pressure to do well?"

He looked over at me with a slight smile on his face and said, "Let me put it this way." *Awesome*, I thought. *He's going to give me the secret to competing in the Olympics! This is what I have been waiting for!* I was more than a little disappointed when he started asking me questions instead. He proceeded, "If I were to place a board that was two feet wide on the ground and asked you to walk across it from one end of this room to the other, could you do it?"

"What does this have to do with the Olympics?" I wanted to ask. Instead, I decided to humor him. I imagined myself walking across a two-foot board very easily, so I nodded. "Could you jog across it?" I thought once again and nodded as before. "Could you sprint across it?" I pictured the board and compared it to a track that I run on at the high school near my house. It would be similar in width, so I replied, "Yeah, I could sprint across it." By this point I was trying to figure out where he was going with this and how it could have anything to do with my questions or the secret to the Olympics.

He nodded, expecting me to reply as I had. Then, after a small pause he leaned over the table closer to me and asked, "Now, close your eyes and imagine that I moved that exact board and placed it 1,000 feet in the air." Immediately I pictured this board reaching across the Grand Canyon as I stood at the edge of the red rock cliffs where the board balanced. I could feel the breeze. I could see what appeared to be a very small river a thousand feet below me. "Could you walk across that board?"

I pictured the two-foot-wide board once again and could only see myself on my hands and knees, crawling very slowly across this board to the other side. "Probably not," I replied.

"Could you jog?" he asked. I shook my head. He continued, "Could you sprint across the board?"

"No," I responded.

"Why not?" Brian asked.

"Because I would be afraid to fall." The same slight smile crossed his face, as though he already knew what my response would be.

He explained, "Exactly. You would be afraid to fall. You would look down and only see the height of the board and the distractions around you, but it would be the exact same board that was across the floor in this room. You said that you would have no problem sprinting across it, and I am asking you to do the exact same thing, with just a change in environment. All you need to do is place one foot in front of the other. When you go to the Olympics, nothing will change except the environment around you. You just need to do what you have come here to do. It is the same process that you have followed in so many competitions before. All you can give is your best, so don't expect more of yourself. Just place one foot in front of the other and focus on where you are going."

Wow. He sure fooled me. It really *was* the secret to competing in the Olympics, and it is one of the many secrets to succeeding in life. Just place one foot in front of the other and focus on where you are going. Learning to focus on where I wanted to go and to eliminate the distractions around me was the key to helping me reach my full potential. Just keep your head up and your eyes looking forward, and place one foot in front of the other.

* * * * * * * *

As I walked into Opening Ceremonies with the rest of my teammates, there was an overwhelming feeling of excitement, accomplishment, and joy. The sacrifice, time, commitment, tears, and determination had all led to this once-in-a-lifetime event. And this single moment made it all worth it. Even while walking into Opening Ceremonies, I continued to tell myself in my mind, *I am an Olympian! I am an Olympian!!* Walking, jumping up and down, laughing, smiling, and waving with the absolute best athletes in the entire world was a dream come true.

When my day of competition came, I remembered the words that Brian had told me: "All you can give is your best, so don't expect more of yourself. Just place one foot in front of the other and focus on where you are going."

I prayed to give my best and to be happy with my effort regardless of where I finished. That Olympic day, I finished fourth. Just so you know, fourth is the absolute worst place to finish. Only the top three get a medal, recognition, and personal validation for being the best athletes in the world. However, I gave myself a pat on the back knowing I had given it my all. I was an Olympian, and no one could ever take that away. My goal was to be an Olympian, and I had become one. My dream came true. I gave it everything I had and did not allow my fears, worries, and doubts to cloud my mind.

We all have fears, worries, negative thoughts, and doubts that creep into our minds, but we must understand that we *always* have a choice to accept these thoughts or push them out. How we feel about ourselves is a direct result of the thoughts that we choose to entertain. How we feel about our circumstances is always a choice. As an Olympic athlete, I have had to become highly aware of my thoughts, and I understand that a very simple thought can be devastating to my performance. I want to challenge you as you go through the next day or week, and eventually the next months and years, to recognize each negative thought that comes to your mind—about yourself, someone else, a project, work, school, any negative thought—and replace it with a positive one. In skeleton, a rookie might slide the course and think, "Don't hit the wall! Oh no, I hit the wall. I'm not very good at this. Don't mess up! I hope they mess up so I can do well. I'm doing everything right, so my equipment must be broken." I promise you, the negative thoughts will hold you back in competition and in life. Olympians and veterans of the sport understand the role of the mind as we strive to think positively. The change is remarkable when we shift our thinking: "Come out two inches to the left. Look center and relax. Nice job, now focus on curve five, and enter three inches to the right. My best will be good enough regardless of what anyone else can do. What can I improve on?"

In life we have a tendency to be distracted by so many things that take our focus off of our ultimate goals and dreams. Just as I would be afraid to fall off of that board once it was placed 1,000 feet in the air, sometimes we lose focus of who we are and where we are going when we pay attention to distracting influences. Women especially seem to naturally have a difficult time loving themselves and staying positive about their self-worth. We might even spend so much time watching the girl on the next board over as she makes her way across that we forget to move our own feet! It is easy to fall into the pattern of comparing others' strengths with our weaknesses. That kind of thinking had caused me to place unrealistic expectations and pressures on myself before my first Olympic competition, and we all sometimes place similar expectations and pressures on ourselves in life. Just as these thoughts and patterns are devastating to an athlete in competition, these habits will only hold us back from becoming our best and reaching our goals.

> "MINE EYES SHALL BE UPON THE, *faithful of the land,* that they may dwell with me: he that **WALKETH** in a **PERFECT WAY, HE SHALL SERVE ME."**
>
> —PSALM 101:6

Be faithful as you move forward. Cheer on, support, and compliment those around you. We have each been blessed with beautiful, unique bodies and talents. We all have weaknesses and we all have strengths. Just as my journey to become an Olympian was challenging at times, this life is also meant to have its share of trials. Remember, all you can give is your best, so don't expect more of yourself. Just place one foot in front of the other and focus on where you are going.

Let's not focus on what's below us. Let us not be afraid to fall but have faith to move forward. Let us reach out to encourage and uplift those around us. Stand tall, keep your head high, and have faith as you place one foot in front of the other.

Once we fill our minds with

positive thoughts about ourselves,

we will be able to more clearly see the *good*

IN THOSE *good* AROUND US.

CHAPTER 9

Useless

Runners

As I took the runners out of my sled, I paused in disbelief. I looked at the runners closely and realized I had made a huge mistake.

People always ask me if I steer my sled. I have had people ask, "Do you just lie there?" or remark, "Wow! You sure are lucky that you got down the fastest!" I can't let myself be bothered by it. If I didn't know what skeleton was and just watched it on TV I would think the same thing. I actually *do* steer my sled down every inch of the track. I know exactly where I want to go and what I need to do to get there. On my sixty-pound sled, there are bars used to steer beneath my shoulders and knees. As the speed increases down the track, the pressures within each curve increase as well. We steer against these pressures. We try to go as straight as we can while driving our sleds the least amount possible in an effort to avoid friction. Any friction on the ice slows us down. I counter the pressures within each curve by pushing down on my opposite knee and shoulder in an effort to torque my sled. This in turn applies pressure to the steel runners (or blades) beneath me as the sled glides across the ice. Confused yet? If you can't tell, skeleton is a pretty technical sport.

We have multiple sets of runners that we fix to the bottom of our sled depending upon the weather and ice conditions. They can make a big difference in our times and results. During the training days that lead up to competitions, athletes switch out their runners to find out which runners will be fastest given the ice conditions and temperatures.

* * * * * * * *

For the final World Cup race just before the 2010 Olympics, a competition was scheduled in the beautiful town of Igls, Austria. It is nestled high in the snow-covered Alps just a few miles from Salzburg, home of *The Sound of Music*. Whenever I compete there, I love rolling down the car window and singing loudly, "The hills are alive with the sound of music!" Janson gets embarrassed and tries to roll my window up before I can hurt anybody else's ears.

Having just been named to the 2010 Olympic roster, I was elated that my dream was finally coming true. I wanted

After crossing the finish line, we set our feet down and drag them along the ice to stop the sled.

everything to be perfect. I wanted to make sure I was ready in every way possible. Because it was the last race left before the Olympics, I wanted to use this World Cup race as a "practice" competition for the Games. I determined to use the same sled, runners, speed suit, helmet, gloves, and shoes that I would compete with at the Olympics in just two short weeks. I wanted to ensure that my confidence was where it needed to be and that everything was prepared and ready to go.

I had been traveling with five different sets of runners. I had tested each set throughout the year. One set that I tested the first week of the season was very slow, and I never pulled those runners out again. The next two sets were decent, but the last two were my favorite sets, and I knew they were faster than any of my others. The weather had been unusually warm in Igls, which was perfect for my desire to use the same runners there that I would use in the warm, coastal climate of Vancouver, Canada.

In preparing for a race we use sandpaper to buff and polish our runners. As we slide down the track, our runners get scratched by dirt, ice crystals, or debris. We want our runners to be as smooth and clean as possible to eliminate even the slightest friction a scratch can cause. We start sanding with a very coarse sandpaper and work our way up to polishing paper that is softer than what you'll find in a bathroom. Preparing runners and a sled for competition can take many hours.

The night before the race I prepared my equipment with care and got into bed. The following morning I woke up bright and early, ready to quite literally take on the world. My best finish of the year was sixth. It wasn't a horrible season, but it wasn't great, either. I really wanted a good result to boost my confidence going into Vancouver.

I stood at the top of the track and tried to imagine the fans that would be present at the Games. I pretended to hear the shouts, bells, and whistles. The Olympic Games represented the moment I had waited and worked so hard for. I wanted to be ready.

I set my sled down, sprinted off the starting block, lunged onto my sled, and focused on each curve ahead. I was very pleased with my performance after two consistent runs. Eager to know the result of my efforts, I strained to see the clock as I crossed the finish line. I finished fifth! I as extremely happy—that was the best result I'd had all year. I had continued to gain speed the entire way down the track, and if it had been longer, I would have medaled. Knowing that the track in the Olympics would be even longer than this track, my expectations soared. I knew I had made some errors, but my runners still allowed me to go fast. Immediately, I jumped off of my sled and gave my coach a hug. He was thrilled with my result as well. I knew that the equipment I raced on that day was exactly what I wanted to compete on in the Olympics.

I returned to my room and began the process of packing my bags yet again for another plane ride. I wanted to ensure that my runners would not be damaged during shipping, so I took them out of my sled and grabbed a different set that I didn't care about to put in their place. As I took the runners out of my sled, I paused in disbelief. I looked at the runners closely and realized I had made a huge mistake. Without looking carefully, I had grabbed the set of runners that early in the season I had determined to be very slow. I had only given them one chance early in the training season, and when I didn't cross the finish in the time that I wanted, I put them away, declaring them to be useless.

This was a great lesson to me about my own perceptions and judgments. Many times we limit our views, possibilities, friendships, and potential because of the faults we determine are present. In dismissing that set of runners the first week of the season, I did not take into consideration the warmth of the ice and its tendency to slow a sled down. I blamed my equipment instead of looking to myself and realizing that I hadn't been on a sled in six months and maybe, just maybe, I wasn't quite comfortable yet or strong enough to put my sled where I wanted it to go. In my mind, there was no way that the problem could possibly be me. So I took those runners and placed them in my case, where they sat unused for five months as I traveled from competition to competition. I had deemed them unworthy of a race and had planned to leave them in my dark, cold basement once I returned home.

Do we sometimes treat or judge others as I had done with my equipment? Do we classify and disapprove of others without giving them a chance?

I believed my equipment was faulty, when in reality, the fault was with me. I'm so grateful that we don't have judges in skeleton racing. In competitions such as figure skating, ski jumping, and aerials, a winner is chosen by the scores they receive from judges who are experts within their sport. If I cross the finish line and I have the fastest time, I win! That's it. Life is not a figure skating competition. We are not experts in anyone else's life, so we shouldn't pretend to be or judge as if we were. I don't even feel that I am an expert in my own life. Every day brings new challenges, experiences, ideas, desires, and emotions that shape me into the person I am. I make plenty of mistakes and strive to learn from them and correct them. We are all doing the best we can.

* * * * * * * *

When I was in junior high, I came across a poem that has stuck with me over the years, "Playing the Game."

There are two aspects to be leery of within the world of judgments. The first is passing judgments, and the second is accepting the judgments that others place upon us. Our lives will never be improved by critiquing, stereotyping, or passing a judgment upon another person. In the moment, we may feel that these thoughts somehow justify our own faults or insecurities. Oftentimes we are guilty of the faults and mistakes that we are so quick to see in others. This isn't news to anyone. Judging others has been a trial for people for thousands of years. Matthew 7:5 rebukes,

"THOU HYPOCRITE, *first cast out the beam out of thine own eye;* **and then shalt thou see clearly** *to cast out the mote out of thy brother's eye."*

"When we try to judge people, which we should not do, we have a great tendency to look for and take pride in finding weaknesses and faults, such as vanity, dishonesty, immorality, and intrigue. As a result, we see only the worst side of those being judged."

—N. ELDON TANNER

Playing the Game

Whatever the game and whatever
   the odds,
The winning is all up to you.
For it isn't the score and it isn't
   the prize
That counts when the playing
   is through.
In the great game of life it's the
   purpose to win
and the courage to fight to the end,
that determines for you what degree
   of success
will be scored to your credit my friend.
The best you can do will be quite enough
To defeat your opponents today;
For you never can lose and you never can fail
If you "put all you've got" in your play.
And the greatest reward that your efforts
   can bring,
Is the fact that you stood to the test,
You played a clean game and you fought
   a good fight,
And you always were doing your best.

Perhaps we may use our negative thoughts about others to build ourselves up and feel better about ourselves, but this pattern inevitably sends us plummeting to the bottom of a mud-filled ditch. Our views of others are a direct result of how we feel about ourselves. Once we fill our minds with positive thoughts about ourselves, we will be able to more clearly see the good in those around us.

We can never fully comprehend, based solely on what we see on the outside, what takes place within another's mind and heart. I was quick to blame my runners and label them slow and useless, when I really needed to look to myself to find areas that needed improving. Once I looked past what I had believed my runners to be, they were given their moment to shine and they helped me to my best result of the season. Give others the benefit of the doubt and allow them to shine.

Recently a study was conducted in which women were given a patch to wear on their arm. The manufacturers claimed that wearing this patch would boost their self-esteem, increase confidence, and make them feel better about themselves and their appearance. After two short weeks, the women were interviewed. They were asked if they felt any different. Every single one of the women claimed the patch had worked. They were more sure of themselves, confident, and happier with their image. After the interviews, the women were told the ingredients of the patch. It was just a sticker, nothing more.

These women believed the patch would improve their lives simply because they were told it would. Consequently, they all noticed that life became better. The choice of how we see ourselves and others is always our own. More often than not, our own assumptions, thoughts, and judgments are very narrow-minded. What we think, whether about ourselves or about those around us, is a direct reflection of our own character.

Wouldn't it be an incredible world if the only thoughts we had about others were positive ones? What if we had a sticker that would empower us to expect greatness from those around us and would encourage us to love them and support them in their efforts to succeed? Imagine if we could truly see past the trendy clothes, the shiny car, the body shape, hairstyle, or makeup and see people for who they could potentially become! How great could we each be if we could let go of worrying about what others think of us or judge us to be? What if we took the time that is usually spent judging or accepting judgments and instead spent it complimenting someone, encouraging a talent, or bettering ourselves?

* * * * * * * *

As an Olympic athlete, I have found that to become my best, I should surround myself with the best. I train with athletes who want to get stronger, and I have coaches who encourage me to excel. I focus on areas that need improving and I am offered help along the way. Surround yourself with positivity. When it can't be found, be the one that brings it out in others. Become the person that others want to surround themselves with in an effort to become their best.

Every little scratch and mark on my runners causes me to slow down. These flaws limit my ability to perform. It takes a lot of time and effort to remove those scratches, but with patience and diligent effort, the runners can be polished and the friction from those scrapes can be eliminated. Judgments cause dirt, ice crystals, and debris to fill our lives and ultimately cause friction. Whether we are passing judgment on others or accepting negative opinions people have about us, we are at risk of slowing down our progress and limiting our ability to grow. Give those around you a chance. Don't stick them in an equipment case and mark them "useless."

I went on to compete in the 2010 Olympic Games, where I had planned to use the runners I had considered to be my fastest set. However, I put them in the case and instead pulled out the set that I had once deemed "slow." They had so much more potential than I had ever believed they would. I raced on my "useless" set, and I finished fourth. It was my best result of the season. These slow runners were actually faster than any other set I had raced on all year. I had missed out on bettering my results over the year because my perception was limited and my judgments were false. Be slow to judge. Give others a chance to excel. We never know what greatness is hidden behind our short-sighted views.

HOPE

GIVES US COURAGE

to do those things

that we don't

believe we are

capable of.

CHAPTER 10

The World
Is Watching

Here I was, four years after

"retirement," competing one last time.

This hadn't been in my

"five-year plan."

Everything came down to this single moment. The world was watching, and I knew it. I had competed a thousand times before, but this was much different. The energy was much higher than in any other competition, the expectations greater, and the pressure on my shoulders heavier than ever. This was the 2014 Olympic Winter Games. This was it. I had one last shot, and then I would walk away from the sport of skeleton and reflect for the rest of my life on this single performance. Our competition consists of sliding down the track four times over two days. I had competed the day before, and I was in second place with two runs to go. As I loaded my sled into the shuttle bus that every athlete had to take to get into the venue, my mind raced and I remembered so many days that led me to this point.

I recalled the one-hour drive to Park City, Utah, over fifteen years ago and taking my first trip in a bobsled at the age of fifteen, when my

Olympic dream began to take flight. Five weeks later I sustained a concussion as the driver hit the roof of a curve and my helmet hit the side of the sled. I persevered. I remembered trying skeleton for the first time. I thought about the sac-

rifices I had had to make. I thought about every party and event I missed my senior year of high school because I wanted to see where my talent would take me. I thought about the sacrifices my parents had made. My friends would get together and hang out while I made the one-hour drive to skeleton practice right after school. I didn't get home until well after dark. I would do my homework, go to bed, and do it all over again the next day. College was extremely busy, to say the least. There were many days when I had to function on only three hours of sleep as I competed in Division I track and field, competing in eight events, took nineteen school credits, and continued to train in the skeleton. While many of my friends were living the college life and enjoying the freedom of being away from home, I strained to dedicate my waking moments to studying and training. Anything great and worth achieving requires sacrifice and motivation. It requires self-control.

The shuttle bus arrived at the top of the track and I carried my sled to the fenced-off area where sleds would be inspected before competition. I walked away, trusting that my equipment was ready to perform,

Every day since Janson and I were married I have continued to think, "It can't get any better than this!"

and went into the start house, where athletes sit and wait for their turn to go.

As I walked into the building, my thoughts drifted to July 12, 2002, when Janson and I were married. He loved and respected me. I thought he was my best friend and that life was at its very best and couldn't get any better. Little did I know that all these years later, thanks to a relationship that we work together at building and strengthening, I'm still thinking the same thing: "It can't get any better than this!" It was so hard to leave for months at a time to compete so soon after we were married. Every trip to the airport meant a tightness in my chest. To help, Janson would write little notes and hide them throughout my suitcases and gear. They always brightened my day.

I set my bags down in the start house, put on my headphones and walked outside once again to begin warming up for the race.

* * * * * * * *

As I walked outside, I remembered a night in a dreary hotel lobby in Sigulda, Latvia. It was December 2004, and I was lying on the burlap-carpeted floor trying to study for a kinesiology final that was due before I went to bed. We had a major World Cup competition early the next morning, but I was committed to school and had promised my professor I would take the test without looking up the answers and turn it in the same day as the rest of the class. My professors were willing to work with me, and I wanted them to know that I was a trustworthy and punctual student. It was the least I could do considering they were willing to work with my absences for competitions. A teammate entered the lobby and asked me why I was studying so long. When I told him I needed to take a test that night, he asked me why I wouldn't just use the book to take the final so that I could prepare for the race. I told him it was a "closed-book test" and he replied with a laugh, "So? Who's gonna know?"

With that, all I could say was, "I will." He shrugged his shoulders and walked away. I continued to study for a few more hours, closed my book, took my final, and got in bed at 2:00 a.m., completely exhausted. Four hours later I woke up, got ready, and went to the track to compete.

Thomas Jefferson once said, "I am sure that in estimating every man's [or woman's] value either in private or public life, pure integrity is the quality we take first into calculation, and that learning and talents are only the second." With relief and

In an effort to see people smiling and having fun during my competitions, I would often write funny sayings or random quotes on my sled. They would say things like, "Keep arms and legs inside vehicle at all times," "It's impossible to lick your elbow," or "Ostriches run 40 miles per hour."

gladness in my mind and heart for my efforts to study and my decision to be honest, I was able to race with a clear conscience. I won the gold medal in that World Cup race in Sigulda—and I later learned that I received an A on my final. Integrity is everything. It is character. It is what you do and who you are.

* * * * * * * *

I began to jog down the outside of the Olympic track, amazed by the architecture of the Russian facilities. It was an evening competition, and the bright orange and pink sunset blazed between the mountain peaks and valleys.

I remembered standing on top of the podium at the end of the 2005 season with my arms high above my head and fists pumping in the air as I became the first U.S. woman to win the Overall World Cup title. Then my thoughts quickly shifted to the tragedy of missing the 2006 Olympics after being hit by a bobsled. The tears, torment, and agony of physical therapy and pushing myself beyond so many limits raced through my mind. Janson had encouraged me to come back. I struggled to do so, but with hope that the next season would be even better than the last, I won the World Championship title just one year later. Hope inspires positive thinking. Hope gives us courage to do those things that we don't believe we are capable of. Hope guides us to look forward to something better.

As I glanced across the mountains my gaze followed the track a mile down the mountainside toward the bottom of the hill, where my family waited for me to cross the finish line.

I recalled the day that Lacee was born and how my perspective on what matters most in life was forever changed. She brought joy and happiness that I never imagined I could feel. Two months after delivering her, I was back in New York racing in the final international competition of the season. I was nervous that I had forgotten how to slide but wanted to see where I was before the long summer break could fill my mind with doubts. I felt like I was in decent shape for having just had a baby until one of my coaches laughed when I put on my speed suit and commented that I had gained a lot of weight. Even knowing that my body was still recovering from pregnancy, it hurt. I had to turn away quickly to hide the tears swelling in my eyes. I competed with determination and finished in second place, with the current World Champion finishing just ahead of me. I was the top U.S. competitor. I learned that when others doubted me, laughed at me, or said something to bring me down, I had to determine to push forward. I learned to be resilient.

* * * * * * * * *

After my warm-up I glanced at my watch. It was time to put on my speed suit and get ready to race. I walked back into the start house and grabbed my backpack. As usual, I took it into the bathroom to change and say a prayer. I thanked Heavenly Father for all of my many blessings and talents. I thanked Him for the opportunity to compete. I prayed that I would be happy with my best, regardless of the result. I asked that the other athletes would be able to do their best as well and that no one would get injured. I prayed to receive peace and comfort before and after the competition. After concluding my prayer, I knew it was all going to work out as it should. I had prepared in every way. I had done absolutely everything I could to deliver my best, so there was little room for doubt. And the little doubts that did enter I pushed away with a positive thought. There was nothing left for me to do except enjoy the moment. I walked out of the bathroom, now in my gear and ready to compete.

The intensity in the room was high, but for some reason I never felt it. I felt extremely calm. I slid my backpack under the bench, sat down, and waited for my turn to go. Turning the music in my headphones up to distract me from the scene around me, I closed my eyes and pictured the day that Janson told me he was going to build me a sled.

My old sled had been severely damaged in shipping to World Championships the year before, and I had to borrow a sled to compete. My results, needless to say, were poor. It was then that my husband said, "I'm going to build you a sled." I laughed and said sarcastically, "Okay." People don't just build sleds. There are maybe five sled builders in the world that I could purchase a sled from. There is a book filled with specific dimensions, shapes, sizes, and rules that need to be strictly adhered to in order to avoid a severe penalty. That next day, right after returning home from work, Janson sat at his computer and began to study the rules and design the perfect sled. Thousands of hours later it was complete, just in time for the 2010 Olympic season. I can't lie—I was doubtful and nervous as I stood at the top of the track to take it down the careening mile-long course. As I crossed the finish line and saw my down time, I couldn't help but be proud of what he had accomplished. The sled was perfect. I vividly remembered crossing the finish line in the 2010 Games and searching for my family in the stands. I had a huge smile on my face and loved seeing the smiles on theirs. I had given it my best. It was perfect. I never did see the scoreboard. Actually, I still don't even know what my times were. I know I finished fourth. I missed a bronze medal by a tenth of a second.

It was time. My teammate gave me a hug, we wished each other luck, and I grabbed my helmet and walked toward the door. I took in a deep breath and let it out slowly as I reviewed the areas of the track that I wanted to improve upon from yesterday's runs. I slid the helmet over my head and clipped the strap beneath my chin in place. I pushed the door open in front of me and was immediately surrounded by cameras and people cheering and shouting.

I had thought I was done after 2010. I actually retired at the ripe old age of twenty-seven, determined never to come back. I didn't want to leave my family anymore. My heart was at home with them, and I couldn't be passionate about competing while they were all thousands of miles away. I remembered when Traycen was born and I couldn't believe how my love expanded and the joy within our family increased. I saw life without skeleton and was happy. Now here I was, four years after "retirement," competing one last time. This hadn't been in my "five-year plan."

I approached the starting line, where Tuffy, my coach, was waiting for me with my sled. He looked more nervous than I felt, so I gave him a pat on the shoulder and said, "Isn't this awesome? This is the Olympics!"

It made us both smile. "Get after it," he replied. Tuffy had been my coach for only the past two years. He taught me how to be a better athlete through the example that he left everywhere he went. He was always positive, encouraging, and serving others. I was glad that he was standing beside me as that green light went off. I focused in on the track ahead, knowing exactly what I needed to do in order to improve upon the runs I had previously taken. I sprinted forward, leaped onto my sled, and navigated my way down the track. Focusing on every inch of the course and reminding myself of the goals I wanted to master, I executed the curves with precision. As I crossed the finish line, I saw that I had made a good time. I have learned that just as the littlest movements I make through-out every inch of the track can add up to a successful run, the smallest decisions we make each day can empower us to achieve greatness.

I knew I still had to make one more run to ensure the result I hoped

for, so I tried not to celebrate too much. My gaze shot to the stands, where I saw my family cheering at the top of their lungs, blowing horns, and waving flags. I was so grateful to have them there with me. I picked up my sled and car-ried it to the back of the truck that would take us up to the top of the track. With gratitude and excitement in my heart for these moments, I thought of the experience that had brought me back to com-pete again.

As I sat in this small truck in Russia waiting for my final run of the Olympic Games, I recalled the extreme pain and sadness our family felt just before making this decision to compete. My "five-year plan" changed drastically one seemingly perfect spring evening in April 2012. Eighteen weeks pregnant with our third child, I had a miscarriage. The doctors had no explanation for it. "Sometimes it just happens," a nurse told me as she walked with us back to our car the following day. I remember the ache in my heart and the frustration over the lack of answers. I examined every little detail of the week leading up to the miscarriage and wondered if I had done something wrong or hadn't done something I should have. A month later, Janson approached me. He knew that I wasn't ready to get pregnant again right away, and he understood that I needed a goal to focus on. He asked if I wanted to go back to skeleton one last time, on the condition that the whole family would travel together. Through faith and prayer, we decided to move forward with our new "five-year plan." We took two steps into the dark, and the light eventually appeared. Miracles happened all along the way. Our faith was tested time and time again. Sometimes it is necessary to hit rock bottom before we can soar to great heights.

✳ ✳ ✳ ✳ ✳ ✳ ✳ ✳

The truck reached the top of the track. The sun had set and the sky was pitch black, but you could still see each mountain in the distance, lit by the luminescent Olympic venues and competitions taking place. Many of the media affiliates had left to station themselves at the bottom of the track to capture the moments of the fourth and final run of competition. The start area was left somewhat desolate. After setting my sled on the inspection rack, I walked into the start house. I received high fives from my coach and trainers. "I still have another run," I would remind them. "One more to go." Pride can lose a race before it even begins.

I had competed on this track in the World Cup test event one year ago and brought home the gold. I remembered how following the race, athletes of another nation had accused me of cheating. We're not allowed to alter the steel runners on our sleds to make them go faster. These athletes would make subtle criticisms in conversations, tell other athletes that I was cheating, and post remarks on social media accusing me of being dishonest. My reputation means a lot to me, but my integrity means everything. It is who I am. I echo the words of Job 27:5:

"*Till I die* I WILL NOT REMOVE MINE INTEGRITY FROM ME."

No amount of medals, fame, or glory could cause me to give up my integrity. I initially wanted to say something harsh or reproving, but I knew that wasn't who I wanted to be either. Then I decided not to do anything and to try to ignore it, but I also wanted to defend my integrity. So I said a prayer. I decided to reply to an accusation on social media, and I simply stated that my integrity is everything to me and I would never do anything to compromise it. I knew I had never cheated to win a medal

or gain recognition before, and I never would in the future. I know who I am and what I stand for regardless of what others say or think. Skeleton is a sport. It is just a sport. My integrity is everything.

* * * * * * * * *

The time passed quickly. Now, just moments before my name would be called for my final run, the only thought and feeling that I had was an overwhelming feeling of gratitude for all of those who had supported me to get to this point. There were so many people who had donated money, time, talents, and abilities that opened this door for me to compete. I called my brother, Rob, who was in Utah watching my race with hundreds of my family and friends that couldn't get to Russia. I wanted to thank them for their love and support. He was shocked by the phone call, and with a laugh in his voice he told me to go get ready.

* * * * * * * * *

Moments later, my name was called. I stood at the starting line ready to go. I gave my coach, Tuffy, a hug; we smiled, he patted my back, and I was off. I could hear him cheering for me as I jumped onto my sled and then—silence. I was so focused on what was in front of me that every shout, cheer, wave, and distraction was eliminated. It felt as though I was the only one within a hundred miles of the track. I could only think one thing at eighty miles per hour with my chin an inch off of the ice: *Faster! Go faster!* We never really know how fast we are going or what our time will be until we cross the finish line and see the result. As I steered my sled through the last curve and saw the finish line ahead, I stretched my neck as far forward as I could. In our sport, we win or lose races by one hundredth of a second, so every little bit helps. Immediately after crossing the finish line I pushed myself up, straining to see the clock. I couldn't see it. I couldn't see anyone. There was a one hundred-meter uphill stretch of track that allowed us to slow down and eventually stop at the finish dock. Time seemed to slow to a snail's pace as I flew up the track and over the crest. *How did I do?! Where did I finish?*

Just then, my previous teammate and current coach and friend, Zach Lund, appeared. He thrust his hands in the air with the biggest smile on his face. It was then that I knew I had just won an Olympic medal. I jumped off of my sled and about knocked him over as I gave him a huge hug. Every emotion I have ever felt was swelling within me. The emotions wanted to burst out of my fingertips and toes and leap out of my chest. More than anything, I wanted to share this moment with my

family in the stands more than twenty feet away. I jumped over the icy wall and onto the asphalt next to the track. Cameras were flashing and the crowd was cheering with exuberance. I looked up to the stands where my family was blocked in the middle of the row. It seemed to me that there was only one way to get to them. I couldn't go around because the aisles were packed with people, so the only option I had was to go straight up. It looked too high to reach. I imagined myself jumping up, missing the railing, and falling flat on my back. With adrenaline rushing through my body and without much thought, I jumped as high as I could and hoped that my hands would grasp something solid. I felt the steel bar of the bleachers in my palms and somehow managed to pull myself up and over the railing to embrace my family. That was right where I wanted to be. It was the most incredible moment as I embraced my kids, knowing that they had sacrificed a lot to make this moment possible. I hugged my siblings and parents with tears streaming down my cheeks. As I reached forward to Janson, all I could say was, "We did it!" It had taken so much for us to achieve this dream. It had taken so many people to make this moment happen. "We did it!"

* * * * * * * * *

Some people have been amazed at my reaction to finishing second. They wonder if I'll continue to slide to try to get that gold medal. Just so you know, I am officially retired from skeleton, and no, I am not going back. The color of a medal does not define who I am. It never has and it never will. I have always loved the scene from the bobsled movie *Cool Runnings* that portrays the coach mentoring his athlete. The coach taught, "Derice, a gold medal is a wonderful thing, but if you're not enough without it, you'll never be enough with it."

Derice then responds, "Hey, coach, how will I know if I'm enough?"

The coach simply states, "When you cross that finish line, you'll know." Following my fourth place finish in Vancouver, I officially knew that I was enough without a medal. I now have a silver medal. The medal is a symbol of the sacrifice, tears, dedication, drive, and goals over the years, but even without that symbol, every experience that has led me to where I am has made me *who* I am, and I am grateful for the journey.

As I looked back through the moments that led to winning the silver medal that Olympic night, I realized that all along, the world was watching. Articles were soon published about experiences from my life or stories that others had to share about me and my character. Someone is always watching. We learn and grow from those around us and the examples that they set. This life is our single moment. It is our time to perform.

I wear a necklace around my neck that has two different pendants. One is a picture of the LDS temple in Salt Lake City, Utah. It reminds

Your good example helps others to find their way in a darkening world. It takes courage to do what you know to be right even when it is hard, very hard. But you will never lose your courage unless you choose to.

—ARDETH KAPP

me to continually progress and be better each and every day. It reminds me of who I am, where I want to go, and who I want to become. The second pendant is an emblem of a torch. It reminds me to be a light. It reminds me to stand up for what I believe regardless of what others might think or do around me. I want to be an example of righteousness and help others to become their best selves. Whether we are on the stage of the world, in a classroom at school, or within the walls of our own home, it is our time to perform. Just as we learn from others' examples, people around us are watching our actions, listening to our words, and learning from us. An incredible woman, Ardeth Kapp, once said, "Your good example

helps others to find their way in a darkening world. It takes courage to do what you know to be right even when it is hard, very hard. But you will never lose your courage unless you choose to." It is our time to be courageous. It's time to become our best selves and set an example for the world to follow so that when all is said and done we can exclaim together, "We did it!"

PHOTO CREDITS